SORRY

Conversations on Election Day
November 6th, 2012

Play 3
The Apple Family
Scenes from Life in the Country

Richard Nelson

BROADWAY PLAY PUBLISHING INC
New York
BroadwayPlayPub.com

First printing: February 2013
Second printing: May 2013
I S B N: 978-0-88145-564-9

Book design: Marie Donovan
Page make-up: Adobe Indesign
Typeface: Palatino
Printed and bound in the U S A

PLAYS BY RICHARD NELSON

Artists In America:
FRANK'S HOME*
FAREWELL TO THE THEATRE
NIKOLAI AND THE OTHERS
(scheduled for production)
THE PECULIAR NATURE OF CITIES
(scheduled for production)

Plays of Adolescence, A Trilogy:
GOODNIGHT CHILDREN EVERYWHERE
FRANNY'S WAY*
MADAME MELVILLE

England/America, A Special Relationship:
SOME AMERICANS ABROAD
TWO SHAKESPEAREAN ACTORS
NEW ENGLAND
WHERE I COME FROM

American History Plays:
COLUMBUS AND THE DISCOVERY OF JAPAN
THE GENERAL FROM AMERICA
HOW SHAKESPEARE WON THE WEST*
CONVERSATIONS IN TUSCULUM

*Published by Broadway Play Publishing Inc

SORRY was commissioned by The Public Theater (Oskar Eustis, Artistic Director; Patrick Willingham, Executive Director). The play opened at the Public Theater on 6 November 2012. The cast and creative contributors were:

RICHARD..Jay O Sanders
BARBARA .... Maryann Plunkett
MARIAN...Laila Robins
JANE... J Smith-Cameron
BENJAMIN..Jon DeVries

Director.. Richard Nelson
Set & costume design....................................Susan Hilferty
Lighting design ....Jennifer Tipton
Sound design...........................Scott Lehrer & Will Pickens
Production stage manager ....Pamela Salling
Stage manager.. Maggie Swing
Production assistant ....Caroline Englander
Assistant director..............................Charlotte Brathwaite
Prop master ....Amelia Freeman-Lynde

CHARACTERS & SETTING

THE APPLES:

RICHARD APPLE, *a lawyer, lives in Brooklyn.*

BARBARA APPLE, *his sister, a high school English teacher, lives in Rhinebeck.*

MARIAN APPLE, *his sister, now a third-grade teacher. Lives in Rhinebeck.*

JANE APPLE HALLS, *his sister, a non-fiction writer, lives in Manhattan with her boyfriend, Tim.*

BENJAMIN APPLE, *his uncle, a retired actor, lives with* BARBARA *and* MARIAN *in Rhinebeck.*

The play takes place between approximately 5 A M and 7 A M on the morning of Tuesday, November 6, 2012.

Rhinebeck, New York; a small historic village one hundred miles north of New York City; once referred to in an article in The New York Times *as "The Town That Time Forgot". A room in* BARBARA APPLE's *house, which she shares with* BENJAMIN *and* MARIAN, *on Center Street.*

Play one: THAT HOPEY CHANGEY THING is set on November 2, 2010. Before the play begins, Uncle Benjamin Apple, a well-known actor, has had a heart attack, which sent him into a coma. When he came out, he had serious amnesia. By the beginning of the play, he has retired, and moved into his niece Barbara's home in Rhinebeck, New York.

Play two: SWEET AND SAD is set on September 11, 2011. Months before the play begins, Marian's twenty-year-old daughter, Evan, committed suicide, for reasons unknown. Since then, Marian and her husband, Adam, have separated, and Marian now shares Barbara's house with Barbara and Benjamin.

"It seems like everyone's asleep."
THREE SISTERS, Chekhov

for
Maryann Plunkett, Laila Robins, J Smith-Cameron,
Jon DeVries, Shuler Hensley, & Jay O Sanders

(A wooden table and four wooden chairs. A few short-stemmed flowers in a small glass bowl on the table. Rugs.)

(Regina Spektor's Fidelity *begins;* BARBARA, *in her robe and nightgown, enters with a tablecloth, which she begins to lay over the table—the tablecloth has been used, stained from a Chinese meal some hours before. [She will reset the flower bowl so that it has fallen over and been forgotten.].)*

(Soon MARIAN *and* JANE, *both in their nightclothes, enter with the remnants of the night-before's meal and post meal—a mostly empty bottle of wine; a bottle of aperitif; a pot of coffee, milk, sugar; a few used cups; a tin of mostly eaten cookies; plates with crumbs; maybe an empty carton of ice cream with a scoop sticking out; a few used ice cream plates, the peels of a tangerine, a few grapes left on their stems in a bowl, trivets. They have been "grazing" at this table for hours.)*

*(*JANE *places two large books on the floor by the table, both left open. And a thin pile of sheet music and other papers on the table.)*

*(*BARBARA *returns with a card table, which she sets up;* MARIAN *returns with a jigsaw puzzle box. After* BARBARA *sets up the card table,* MARIAN *pours the puzzle pieces out; and turns over a few of them. Little has been done on this puzzle.)*

(It is five in the morning, November 6, 2012. No one has gone to bed.)

(The general sense that the sisters have been hanging out in here all night.)

(BARBARA *takes off her robe, drapes it over the back of a chair, sits at the puzzle and lights come up:*)

Shape-Note Singing

(BARBARA *is at the puzzle.* JANE *and* MARIAN *at the table.*)

(JANE *is looking at some sheet music.*)

(*Church bells in the distance toll five.*)

(JANE *follows the piece of sheet music [*BARBARA *and* MARIAN *know the piece] and is in the middle of singing to herself:*)

JANE: fa fa sol fa...

BARBARA: (*Over the puzzle, to* MARIAN) I remember when Jane was something like five years old, and we were all doing a puzzle at Thanksgiving. And there was one piece—Part of a red scarf. I really wanted to find that piece. Uncle Benjamin said he'd give me a quarter if I found it. I didn't move for hours from that puzzle. But no one could find it. So we finished the whole puzzle, except for that one piece and it was in the middle, and then Uncle winked at Jane, and Jane you leaned down and lifted up a corner of the rug under the card table, and then smiling you said— "oh, look I've found the last piece."

(*Then:*)

JANE: (*Looking at the sheet music, "innocently"*) I don't remember that.

(BARBARA *and* MARIAN *exchange a look.*)

JANE: (*Continuing to follow the music*) sol sol fa fa fa

MARIAN: (*To* JANE) The incredible thing with shape-note singing— (*Turns to* BARBARA)

BARBARA: What?

MARIAN: *(To Jane about* BARBARA*)* She doesn't really like this kind of—

BARBARA: I do. It's just different. I like it. It's hard. But I like it.

MARIAN: *(Over the end of this, to* JANE*)* The student conductor he gave us a talk.

BARBARA: *(To* JANE*)* They have students conduct at Bard. They teach that.

JANE: You've told me.

BARBARA: *(Over this)* We're like their "guinea pigs". Marian said, like their "cadavers".

JANE: *(To* MARIAN*)* What sort of talk?

MARIAN: How these songs--. They're not meant to be *performed* for anyone.

BARBARA: Marian, I like the longer pieces. I like the Mozart we're doing. I just like that better.

(Shrugs)

JANE: *(To* MARIAN*)* I don't understand. What do you mean?

MARIAN: He told us— *(To* BARBARA*)* —let's sing one, Barbara. Show her.

JANE: Told you what?

MARIAN: In shape-note singing, you're supposed to get in a circle. And everyone just sings. No one can just listen. You're not allowed to do that. *(To* BARBARA*)* Right?

*(*BARBARA *nods.)*

MARIAN: You can't just stand on the sidelines. There is no *audience*. It's not *for* anyone. We sing with each other. To each other. For ourselves. *(To* BARBARA*)* You can't just sit and watch. Did I explain it right?

(She nods.)

MARIAN: *(To* JANE*)* He did say one thing that was very interesting. *(To* BARBARA*)* Didn't he?

JANE: What?

MARIAN: *(Over this)* He said—he imagined these "pioneers", say in the wilderness, in the middle of nowhere, in a storm. They don't know what's going to happen. Anything could happen. What the night will bring. The roof of their cabin feels like it's about to blow off. Or cave in. That's what it feels like. They can imagine the worst. And the family, and whoever else happens to be there—sheltering—so maybe neighbors, or maybe just the family—they all get together in a circle, face each other and sing. That's how he imagines it. The student conductor. And as loud as they can sing. Loud seems to be a big part of it. The louder the better. As if that would ward off any evil, I suppose. Just the act of the singing together. And that—was all they had left… *(Short pause)* Barbara?

BARBARA: Which one?

*(*MARIAN *choosing a piece of sheet music:)*

MARIAN: "As we travel…"

*(*MARIAN *hands* JANE *the sheet music to follow.)*

BARBARA: *(Still doing the puzzle, starts to sing)* As we travel through the—

MARIAN: *(To* JANE*)* And it doesn't matter how well you sing.

BARBARA: *(Stopping doing the puzzle)* Marian's been in the chorus three months and she's already one of the favorites. No one still even notices me.

MARIAN: That's not true. That is not true. *(To* JANE*)* We know that isn't true, Barbara…

BARBARA: *(Sings)*
As we travel through the desert
Storms beset us by the way.
But beyond the river Jordon
Lies a field of endless day.

(MARIAN joins in for the chorus.)

BARBARA & MARIAN:
Farther on, still go farther
Count the milestones one by one.

MARIAN: *(Pointing out to JANE)* We changed the "Jesus"
to "we".

JANE: Why?

MARIAN: *(It's obvious)* It's Bard College.

BARBARA & MARIAN:
We will forsake you never.
It is better farther on.

(BARBARA now leaves the puzzle table and joins her sisters at the table. They are getting into this.)

MARIAN: *(Pointing to the place)* Jane.

JANE: *(Hesitates, then sings)*
Oh, my brother are you weary
Of the roughness of the way?

(BARBARA and MARIAN help JANE, support her.)

JANE: Does your strength begin to fail you
And your vigor to decay?"

BARBARA, JANE & MARIAN: *(BARBARA and MARIAN come
in with the chorus: very loud and joyous)*
Farther on, still go farther
Count the milestones one by one.
We will forsake you never.
It is better farther on."

MARIAN: *(To* JANE, *point out)* That's an oval. There. So it's "sol".

BARBARA & MARIAN: *(Sing the melody together, they've obviously practiced this and are having fun. [note they are not singing into the meaning of the lyric, but the opposite, joyous])*
At my grave, oh still be singing
Though you weep for one that's gone."

*(*BARBARA *and* MARIAN *urge* JANE *to join, she does hesitantly and in and out)*

BARBARA & MARIAN:
Sing it as we once did sing it.
(Loud) It is better farther on.

BARBARA, JANE & MARIAN:
Farther on, still go farther
Count the milestones one by one.
We will forsake you never
It is better farther on."

(They finish—laughing, having enjoyed that a great deal.)

MARIAN: *(As they laugh)* We rehearse it all the time. *(Listing)* When we do the dishes.

BARBARA: *(The list)* The laundry. We've even had Benjamin singing it during the hurricane.

MARIAN: *(Then)* He tried.

(As they settle down.)

JANE: When's the concert?

MARIAN: *(To* BARBARA*)* Three weeks?

BARBARA: *(Same time, feeling the coffee pot)* About a month. *(Getting up)* Maybe I should put on more coffee. This is cold. We're not going to bed.

JANE: No. *(About the concert)* I should come up and see it.

MARIAN: *(Getting up, about the coffee)* I'll do it. You'd
like it I think, Jane. And Tim could sing in the chorus
too.

JANE: You know I think he'd really like to do that. He's
almost said as much.

MARIAN: They should be so lucky. *(To* BARBARA*)* You
know tonight's chorus night.

BARBARA: I'd forgotten.

MARIAN: That'll be nice. Won't it? It'll be nice to be
singing tonight. *(She goes into the kitchen)*

*(*BARBARA *sits and sighs.)*

BARBARA: *(To* MARIAN*)* I'll need that.

JANE: *(Joking)* Maybe we all will...

*(*BARBARA *looks at* JANE*.)*

JANE: *(Seriously)* It's the right thing to do, Barbara.
We all know that. There is absolutely nothing to feel
guilty about. It's the only thing to do. Give him time.
Benjamin will see this— *(too)*

BARBARA: *(Hearing a noise, over the end)* What's that?

MARIAN: *(Off, calls)* Jane! Could you come in here,
please! I need your help!

JANE: What does she need my help—? *(She gets up.)*

BARBARA: I don't know. I don't know.

JANE: *(Hesitates, then)* Coming...I'm coming...

*(*JANE *goes.* BARBARA *sits at the table, suddenly lost in her
thoughts.)*

(Lights fade.)

Barbara and Benjamin

(A short time later. BARBARA *still at the table, her back to the kitchen door.)*

(From the kitchen comes RICHARD, *followed by his sisters. He is gesturing to them not to make a noise. He is "tiptoeing".* JANE *goes around the table so she will be able to see* BARBARA's *face.)*

*(*RICHARD *approaches* BARBARA *from behind. As he grabs her shoulder:)*

RICHARD: I need your vote!!

*(*BARBARA *screams:)*

BARBARA: What?!! *(She is shaken.)*

JANE: *(Trying to calm her)* It's Richard.

MARIAN: *(Over this)* Richard's here early.

BARBARA: *(Over this, gasping for breath, to Richard, very upset)* What? Oh fuck you! Fuck you, Richard! Jesus Christ.

RICHARD: What did I do?

BARBARA: Don't you ever do that to me!

MARIAN: I told him you weren't going to like it.

JANE: *(To* BARBARA*)* I told him too.

RICHARD: I'm sorry. *(To* JANE*)* You thought it would be—

BARBARA: *(To* RICHARD*)* Fuck you. What the hell are you doing? You scared the hell out of me.

RICHARD: I didn't mean—

JANE: *(To* RICHARD*)* What were you thinking?

RICHARD: I—

BARBARA: For Christ sake! *(Calming a little:)* It's five in the morning. You're not supposed to be—

RICHARD: I know. I came early. Was that wrong?

BARBARA: *(Over the end of this)* It's not time to take Benjamin yet. They're not ready for him—

MARIAN: *(Over the end of this)* I told him not to. *Jane* thought it'd be funny.

RICHARD: I didn't think I'd scare you that much.

BARBARA: *(Takes a big deep breath)* My god...Jesus. So— how are you Richard? Welcome home.

RICHARD: I'm fine. Nice to be here. Nice to be welcomed with open arms.

BARBARA: It's like five in the morning.

RICHARD: I know. I'm sorry, Barbara. Get over it. Nice to see you too.

BARBARA: Now you're pissed at me?? *(To her sisters)* That doesn't seem fair. Does it?

(Neither wants to answer that.)

BARBARA: What are you doing here?

RICHARD: You asked me to come as soon as I got back—

BARBARA: I mean right now. At five in the fucking morning.

RICHARD: Language, Barbara.

JANE: *(Over this)* He said he's jet-lagged. *(To* RICHARD*)* She's a little on edge.

BARBARA: I'm not— "on edge". Let's start again. Welcome home, Richard. We've been waiting for you.

*(*BARBARA *and* RICHARD *hug.)*

(Then:)

RICHARD: By the way, I haven't had breakfast.

JANE: Who are you saying this to?

MARIAN: There's the kitchen.

RICHARD: Come on, I've been staying in a hotel for two months, I've gotten used to someone making me breakfast.

MARIAN: Is he serious?

JANE: And what does your wife say about that?

RICHARD: I haven't told her yet. *(Then)* I'm joking. It was a joke.

MARIAN: No, you're not. He's not.

JANE: No.

RICHARD: I can get my own breakfast. I assume that's all right? I'll get it. I'm sorry I'm early, Barbara. And I'm sorry I made a joke. I just woke up. Pamela rolled over and took one look at me and said—go to your sisters. *They* can't wait to see you. *(Smiling)* I guess she was wrong.

(RICHARD laughs. No response to that)

MARIAN: *(To* JANE*)* It wasn't a joke.

RICHARD: I'd thought I'd wait in the car. I wasn't going to wake you. But the lights were on.

BARBARA: Everybody's up.

RICHARD: I can see that. And why is everyone up?

JANE: I don't know why I'm doing this—but I'll get your damn breakfast.

RICHARD: I'm not asking—

BARBARA: There's a stale bagel in the bread box.

RICHARD: That's fine. I'm happy with that! Anything stale is fine.

JANE: You are so spoiled, Richard. He always was.

(JANE "smacks" RICHARD on the stomach, he pretends to smack her back—something they did as kids.)

JANE: How do you want your eggs?

MARIAN: He likes them scrambled.

JANE: Why did I know that too? *(To* RICHARD*)* Do you know how I like my eggs?

MARIAN: *(To* RICHARD*)* Do you?

(No response from RICHARD. JANE *starts to go.)*

JANE: You still can't drink grapefruit juice?

RICHARD: I can't. I wish I could, but I can't.

*(*JANE *goes into the kitchen. Awkward pause)*

RICHARD: I am very sorry, Barbara, that I scared you so much. *(He touches the coffee pot.)*

MARIAN: It's cold. She'll get you coffee too. Just like a hotel. Sit down.

*(*RICHARD *sits,* BARBARA *and* MARIAN *begin to straighten up the table:)*

BARBARA: *(Explaining the mess)* We've been up all night.

MARIAN: *(Nodding toward where* JANE *exited)* Tim's in Chicago. *(Amazed:)* He got a part in a play.

RICHARD: He e-mailed me—

MARIAN: Someone pulled out at the last second.

RICHARD: He sounded excited.

MARIAN: *(Over half of this)* He already knew the part. Jane said he had to pay his own way out there.

RICHARD: Why would he have to do that—?

BARBARA: How was the flight?

RICHARD: Fine.

BARBARA: And the kids? Pamela said they loved getting out of school last week.

RICHARD: I saw them for like two seconds. You said you needed me here the moment I got back, Barbara-

(BENJAMIN *has appeared in yesterday's clothes, stocking feet; this stops* RICHARD.)

BARBARA: It's Richard.

BENJAMIN: I know it's Richard.

RICHARD: Benjamin.

BENJAMIN: How do you do, son?

BARBARA: He's your nephew.

BENJAMIN: I know.

(BARBARA *looks at* RICHARD. BENJAMIN *sees this.*)

BENJAMIN: (*To* BARBARA, *very insistent*) I know it's Richard!

(RICHARD *is surprised by this. He shares a look with* MARIAN.)

MARIAN: He was just in England for months, Uncle.

RICHARD: Two. Two months.

MARIAN: We haven't seen him for two months.

(BENJAMIN *looks at* RICHARD, *then:*)

BARBARA: You worked a lot in England, Benjamin.

BENJAMIN: Did I?

RICHARD: Good to see you, Uncle. Very good to see you. You're looking well.

(RICHARD *goes to hug* BENJAMIN, *but stops, they shake hands, awkward moment.* RICHARD *tries to laugh it off.*)

MARIAN: Benjamin's been watching his own movies. It's been an all-night marathon. Hasn't it? How many of your movies did you end up watching, Uncle? (*To* RICHARD) We gave up after three… (*Then*) Who else wants breakfast? Jane's making Richard eggs.

BENJAMIN: What about dinner? I've been waiting forever for dinner.

BARBARA: *(A little fed up)* We had dinner, Benjamin. It's five almost five thirty in the morning.

BENJAMIN: I didn't have any dinner.

(MARIAN and RICHARD share a look: "see what it's been like?" then:)

MARIAN: We had Chinese food. From your favorite place. China Rose? You went with me to pick it up. *(To RICHARD)* We stood on their patio and looked at the river. *(To BENJAMIN)* And you had a smoke? *(To RICHARD)* Barbara had cooked him a whole dinner—

BARBARA: His favorite.

MARIAN: Then he wanted take out...

BARBARA: I don't care.

BENJAMIN: Where's the Chinese food?

MARIAN: *(To BARBARA)* Cold?

BARBARA: *(Shrugs)* Cold. *(To BENJAMIN)* Okay?

BENJAMIN: It's from my favorite place?

MARIAN: You want chop sticks Uncle? *(Goes without waiting for an answer, passing JANE)*

BARBARA: *(About the mess)* Maybe I should... We've been up all night.

RICHARD: You said.

(BARBARA begins again to clear things.)

JANE: What do you want with your eggs, Richard?

RICHARD: I don't need anything else.

JANE: Barbara has bagels. They're fresh. And there's cereal.

(RICHARD is watching BARBARA.)

JANE: I'll get cereal. Barbara has all kinds of cereal.

BARBARA: *(Correcting her)* Barbara and Marian...

RICHARD: I don't care… *(He has stood up again:)* Shouldn't we sit down at the table, Uncle?

(BENJAMIN looks to BARBARA.)

(JANE goes back into the kitchen.)

BARBARA: *(Touching BENJAMIN on the shoulder)* Sit down with Richard.

(BENJAMIN shakes her hand off of him. RICHARD watches this. He "sees" the puzzle.)

RICHARD: Who's been doing a puzzle?

BARBARA: We keep giving up.

RICHARD: You've hardly done anything. *(Big smile)* You need me!

BARBARA: You were never any good at puzzles, Richard.

RICHARD: *(Ignores her, looks at the box, reads:)* "The Luncheon of the Boating Party." I didn't know you liked puzzles, Uncle.

(Short pause)

BARBARA: *(Suddenly as she goes into the kitchen)* I'll help bring things in…

RICHARD: If eggs are a problem—

BARBARA: What about an egg roll? *(She is gone.)*

(BENJAMIN and RICHARD are alone.)

RICHARD: *(To say something)* You look good.

BENJAMIN: Thank you.

(Then:)

RICHARD: Rhinebeck seems to have dodged the bullet.

BENJAMIN: A bullet?

RICHARD: The hurricane. I think I saw like one tree down.

BENJAMIN: Uh-huh.

(Then:)

RICHARD: I just got home. Last night about five. *(Smiles)*
Stupidly I turned on the T V. *(Smiles, then:)* All the
noise, right? Doesn't it drive you crazy? You must
really be sick of it.

BENJAMIN: Of what?

RICHARD: The noise. The election. I'm really happy I've
been away for two months. *(Then:)* A lot of lawn signs
out in Rhinebeck. I noticed that right away. Even in
the dark—. There seems to be a guy running up here
named "Gibson" with a "b"'. And another guy running
named "Gipson" with a "p". *(Smiles)* I suppose that's a
difference...

BENJAMIN: *(Gestures)* Could I have some wine?

RICHARD: *(Looks toward the kitchen)* Is that all right?

(RICHARD changes the subject. BENJAMIN just looks at him.)

RICHARD: I don't think I could vote for Gillibrand even
if my life depended upon it. *(Smiles)* Don't they trust
us to have elections in New York anymore? Thank you,
Mister Schumer.

*(BARBARA and MARIAN return with glasses, orange juice,
plates, etc.)*

RICHARD: Benjamin wants some wine.

*(Without hesitating, BARBARA reaches and takes the bottle
and hands it to RICHARD.)*

BARBARA: *(As she picks up a glass, to BENJAMIN)* I think
this is your glass.

(BARBARA sets it on the table, RICHARD pours.)

BARBARA: *(To RICHARD)* Good flight?

RICHARD: You already asked that.

BARBARA: *(Not listening)* I'll bet Pamela and the kids were happy to see you.

RICHARD: *(Handing* BENJAMIN *his wine)* I brought gifts. *(Smiles)* To make sure.

BARBARA: I'm sure that was the only reason.

RICHARD: That was a joke.

BARBARA: Pamela said on the phone the kids were driving her crazy. What with no school.

(BENJAMIN has sat at the table.)

BENJAMIN: Where's the Chinese food?

MARIAN: It's coming.

RICHARD: *(Smiles)* I was eager to see all of you.

BARBARA: *(Setting the table)* You going to sit there? We expected you around ten.

RICHARD: Where do you want me to sit?

BARBARA: I don't care.

RICHARD: I woke up, Barbara… You want me to go out, drive around Rhinebeck and come back at ten? I'm sorry.

(BARBARA sits down at the card table.)

(RICHARD looks at BARBARA and at BENJAMIN. He turns to MARIAN:)

RICHARD: How's school?

(RICHARD watches BENJAMIN drink his wine.)

MARIAN: I'm teaching third grade this year. So I have a lot of the same kids as last year. That's mostly good.

BARBARA: Marian's talking about quitting teaching.

RICHARD: *(To MARIAN)* You've talked like that before. What would you do?

(JANE enters with some bagels, cereal, etc.)

JANE: What are we talking about? *(She sets out food.)*

BARBARA: *(To say something:)* Tim's trying to convince Jane to move to Rhinebeck.

JANE: He is.

RICHARD: *(To BARBARA)* She mentioned this in an email. I think she has some concerns about this. Jane's a city girl, aren't you?

BARBARA: Tim's trying to get his daughter full time. That's a lot to ask of Jane.

(MARIAN moves the milk pitcher to RICHARD.)

MARIAN: This is skim. It's all we're allowed to have in the house now.

RICHARD: *(To BARBARA)* What do you mean?

MARIAN: Karen's been up three, four times. She's a terrific kid. Ten years old. I love that age. All downhill after that. *(Smiles)* I've given her some of Evan's old toys and books and things. *(Smiles)*

JANE: And clothes. You kept everything.

RICHARD: I'm sure Karen liked that.

JANE: *("Are you crazy? Of course":)* She's ten years old. *(To BARBARA:)* You going to have breakfast? It seems like we're having breakfast. I'll get you the cold Chinese food, Uncle.

BENJAMIN: Thank you.

(JANE goes. RICHARD starts to eat.)

(BARBARA and MARIAN sit and begin to pick at things as:)

BARBARA: Richard, when Benjamin was filming one of his movies... *(To BENJAMIN)* Right?

BENJAMIN: What—?

BARBARA: We watched it tonight. You told us about this. Sometimes it just comes out of him, Richard. You think he doesn't remember and then...

BENJAMIN: What movie?

(BARBARA *tries to take* BENJAMIN'*s hand, he won't let her.* RICHARD *watches this closely.*)

BARBARA: You're in a big water tank—like a swimming pool. Only much bigger. The *Columbus* movie, Benjamin.

(JANE *returns with the Chinese food, still in the little white containers.*)

BARBARA: When you were in Malta. *(To the others)* He did that whole movie in Malta. *(To* BENJAMIN*)* You were telling us about it tonight. *(To* JANE*)* Wasn't he? *(To* BENJAMIN*)* And...? Come on.

MARIAN: Barbara...

BARBARA: He knows it. He does.

BENJAMIN: The Director?

BARBARA: That's right! That's right. *(She's very pleased, too pleased, then to* RICHARD:*)* That's right. It's very funny. He has so many amazing stories.

RICHARD: He always did.

BENJAMIN: The director..

BARBARA: And...? And what? *(Prompting him:)* He's in a little boat. Remember? With a megaphone. In the big water tank. In Malta!

MARIAN: Barbara—

BARBARA: *(To* BENJAMIN*)* And you said he shouts back through his megaphone to all of you actors gathered on the side of the ship. *(To* RICHARD*)* The *Santa Maria*. He remembered that earlier tonight. He just remembers. A lot more than you think.

BENJAMIN: He says…

BARBARA: Go ahead. You remember.

BENJAMIN: Says…

BARBARA: *(Jumps in)* "O K, body in the water. All very sad. All very sad. All very sad." He's telling them to act very sad. *(She "laughs".)*

BENJAMIN: "All very sad."

BARBARA: Then, what? "Shark! Horrible!" And you're all supposed to now act "feel horrible".

(BARBARA laughs. RICHARD forces a smile.)

RICHARD: That's very funny, Uncle.

(They pass food around.)

JANE: *(To BENJAMIN, pointing out)* Moo shu pork. Egg rolls in there. I ate all the vegetarian ones. Sorry. *(To RICHARD)* I'll get your eggs. *(She goes.)*

RICHARD: So that was one of the movies you were just watching? The Columbus movie?

BENJAMIN: *(Checking out the Chinese)* I don't know.

(RICHARD looks to MARIAN who nods.)

RICHARD: I liked that movie. Didn't we all see that together? At the Ziegfield, I think.

MARIAN: I saw it in Kingston at the mall. With Adam.

RICHARD: Maybe it was just Jane and *her* husband.

MARIAN: It wasn't me.

BARBARA: *(Another effort to engage BENJAMIN:)* He likes to watch them over and over. He seems endlessly fascinated by himself. *(She is trying to tease him:)* Aren't you? Actors...

(BARBARA smiles. BENJAMIN ignores her.)

(BARBARA starts to serve BENJAMIN, putting the food on a plate.)

(JANE enters with the eggs as:)

BENJAMIN: *(Pushing her hand away, and a bit harsh)* I can do it.

(This is noticed by all, especially RICHARD.)

MARIAN: *(To RICHARD)* He's tired.

BARBARA: *(To BENJAMIN)* Of course you can.

(As she watches BENJAMIN serve himself, spilling a little on the table cloth.)

BARBARA: Someone in town asked Uncle if he wanted to be in *A Christmas Carol* this year. Didn't they? *(About the table cloth)* It's dirty already. *(She moves a box closer to help him.)* To play the Ghost of Christmas Future. That part doesn't have any lines. But it's a good role. Very good. People here in Rhinebeck, they know all he's done. We even went to one rehearsal. *(She is serving him now.)* You could tell it was a big thing for them. Benjamin Apple being there. Someone even asked for his autograph. And he was—amazing.

RICHARD: I'll bet.

BARBARA: Incredible. Scared the living daylights out of Scrooge and all of us. Didn't you? Just by the looks he gave. *(Smiles at BENJAMIN)*

RICHARD: I can picture it.

JANE: I forgot the jelly— *(She starts to go.)*

RICHARD I don't need—

BARBARA: Then—he wouldn't go back.

(JANE stops to listen.)

BARBARA: I told him he can still rehearse every weekend. This doesn't change that. He's going to be here every weekend. I don't think he understands that,

Richard. Maybe you can help. Maybe he'll listen to you. I've promised to pick him up every Friday after I finish school.

JANE: *(Gently)* Talk to him, Barbara.

BARBARA: I have!

(This stops everyone, then:)

BARBARA: Beacon's only forty-five minutes away. Fifty in traffic. And he can spend Friday night, and all day Saturday and most of Sunday. The Rhinebeck theater society was fine with that. *(Then)* The Ghost of Christmas Future is only in a couple of scenes. *(As a joke:)* And he already knows his lines. *(Smiles)*

(BENJAMIN reaches for his glass of wine.)

BARBARA: *(As she pushes it away)* It's morning, Uncle. You don't really want that, do you?

BENJAMIN: *(Explodes)* Will you fucking leave me alone?!!

(Pause)

RICHARD: *(Stunned, confused)* Benjamin!??

JANE: *(To RICHARD)* Leave it, Richard. *(Then:)* How was London?

(Lights fade.)

Ideas for Jane

(A short time later, RICHARD, as he eats, is in the middle of a story. The sisters start to have their own ad hoc breakfasts from what's on the table.)

(BENJAMIN eats his Chinese dinner out of the boxes.)

RICHARD: So Pierce knows he's made this promise to his wife—never to run for political office again. She got him to agree to that. To swear an oath. She just couldn't stand being a politician's wife.

JANE: Understandable. Certainly today.

MARIAN: *(To* JANE*)* I know. Once Adam said he was going to run for the Assembly—

JANE: When was this?

BARBARA: Marian, let him tell his story.

RICHARD: It's— *(fine)*

JANE: I'll bet if you asked Michelle Obama—

RICHARD: *(To* JANE*)* I don't know about that. I used to think that...

JANE: When he decided to run the first time.

RICHARD: *(To the table)* Was she *really* like that?

MARIAN: I told Adam no.

BARBARA: Go on with your story, Richard.

*(*RICHARD *looks to* MARIAN *and* JANE.*)*

JANE: Go ahead. I'm listening.

(Then:)

RICHARD: So how was Pierce now going to explain to his wife that—that he'd just been nominated by his party for President?! Of course he'd been hoping for this. He'd maneuvered behind the scenes to get this. And of course behind his wife's back. Because he'd promised her. Now the convention had nominated him, so... He has to tell her—something. What could I do? He says. They're forcing me, Jane. *(To* JANE*)* She was a Jane too. *(Continues)* He says this. She looks at him—and supposedly says something like—if you're lying to me, Franklin Pierce, may the wrath of God come down upon your head, and God have mercy on your soul... *(Sips his orange juice)* She really didn't want to be a politician's wife.

JANE: *(The most obvious thing in the world)* No.

RICHARD: Anyway, then he wins the presidency.

MARIAN: This is when again? I know nothing about—

JANE: *(Over this)* 1850s?

RICHARD: Fifty two. *(Continues)* And it's so obvious that he's pleased and that he wanted this. He can't hide that from her. And so by now she knows that he'd lied. Even though he swore to God—he'd lied.

MARIAN: I know nothing absolutely nothing about Franklin Pierce.

JANE: Who does?

RICHARD: That's why I think, for Jane, this could be interesting.

JANE: Keep going. *(To her sisters)* I am looking for what to write next.

(Then:)

RICHARD: So he wins. And then—

MARIAN: What?

RICHARD: His nightmare begins. That's what's so chilling.

(BARBARA has been looking at BENJAMIN.)

BARBARA: *(To RICHARD)* What were you saying?

RICHARD: Remember what his wife said, if you break your promise: may the wrath of god and so forth. Okay. That is just what seems to have happened.

JANE: What do you mean?

MARIAN: Let him tell us, Jane. *(To BARBARA)* I love the way Richard tells a story.

BARBARA: You love the way Richard does anything.

MARIAN: That's not true. That is not true.

RICHARD: So before Pierce is even sworn in, before the inauguration and everything, during the transition, Franklin and Jane, they're on a train from Boston to—Andover, Mass. With them is their son, Benji. *(Looks to* BENJAMIN*)* Benjamin. *(Continues)* Eight years old, I think. It's a beautiful sunny day in Massachusetts. When all of a sudden—for no apparent reason—maybe it hits something? Anyway the two-car train just tips over and rolls down an embankment, does a complete somersault, three hundred and sixty degrees. Right off the tracks. And lands, right side up. Like nothing had happened. Like a dream. The train now sits in a corn field. All the passengers were of course shook up, but not one was even scratched—except for young Benji.

MARIAN: What happened?

RICHARD: As the two railroad cars flipped, it seems one chair or seat got loose and thrown into the air, and it hit Benji. In the head. With incredible force. In front of his mother and father—the now President-elect of the United States, Benji to their utter horror, was struck, and—decapitated.

MARIAN: Oh my god.

JANE: Jesus.

*(*BENJAMIN *is listening too now.)*

RICHARD: In front of their eyes. Jane of course was inconsolable, who wouldn't be. Franklin tries to comfort her or maybe himself, but she suddenly gets it into her head that this must be God's wrath, His punishment upon them for Franklin having lied. And sworn. *(Then:)* Jane convinced herself of this. Nothing he or anyone else could say could change her mind. Pretty soon they have to start to make their way to Washington for the inauguration. Jane Pierce makes it as far as Baltimore, where she just stopped, refused to go any farther, or closer to that evil city—of lying

politicians: Washington. Franklin finds friends there
with whom she can stay. And she will spend the next
two and a half years—the bulk of Pierce's Presidency,
in Baltimore, trying, she said to make amends with
God, and writing letters to herself, and all of which she
signs— "Benji".

(Short pause. They eat.)

MARIAN: Poor woman.

BARBARA: *(To* BENJAMIN*)* Interesting, isn't it, Benjamin?

*(*BENJAMIN *ignores* BARBARA.*)*

RICHARD: Pierce of course had no choice but to
continue on his own to Washington, in full mourning
now, not just for his son, but also for his wife. The balls
are cancelled. There are no parties. *(Then:)* And then
one more thing—and because of this rumors start to
fly that maybe this is God's punishment. *(Then:)* The
newly elected Vice President, Franklin is now told—
his name was King, is in Havana. And he's not going
to make the inaugeration. He's in excruciating pain.
Various of his appendages have turned black and are
falling off. And soon he dies in Cuba. Syphilis. *(Then:)*
And so, Franklin Pierce began his presidency.

(Short pause)

JANE: And we think Obama had a rough beginning.

MARIAN: Joe Biden's fingers and toes weren't falling
off.

JANE: I'm not sure it was just the fingers and toes,
Marian.

*(*JANE *looks at* RICHARD *and smiles: about* MARIAN.*)*

MARIAN: What? I don't understand. You mean…?

RICHARD: I knew nothing about this. Nothing. As I
said I just happened across this book—in a stall under
Waterloo Bridge. *(To* JANE*)* So I don't know if it's a

biography of Jane Pierce... Or about their marriage? Or his first hundred days. I don't know. You said you're looking for ideas for your next book.

JANE: I am—

(BENJAMIN has stood up. All look at him.)

JANE: All done, Uncle?

BARBARA: Enjoy your Chinese food?

(After a look at BARBARA, BENJAMIN goes off toward his room and the conversation changes.)

MARIAN: *(To BARBARA)* Is he going to change? *(To RICHARD)* He's been wearing that since yesterday. *(To sisters)* We should get dressed too sometime.

RICHARD: What time are we going?

MARIAN: *(To RICHARD)* We took the day off school.

RICHARD: You told me you were going to do that. Was that a problem?

JANE: I can't stand watching this. It's so unfair to you, Barbara. It really is.

RICHARD: I didn't know this was going on.

MARIAN: I told—

RICHARD: Not like this. *(To BARBARA)* He blames you?

MARIAN: When he remembers.

RICHARD: I'm sorry, Barbara.

BARBARA: I thought we said we'd go *late* morning. Isn't that what we said?

MARIAN: They expect us around eleven, I think. I'm sure we can go earlier. I think we were just waiting for Richard, weren't we?

RICHARD: *(To BARBARA)* What does he understand?

MARIAN: *(After realizing* BARBARA *is not going to answer)*
Sometimes—everything. You'd be amazed. Then he
forgets, and—is happy.

BARBARA: *(Standing, to pick up* BENJAMIN's *plate)* Why
do we have to get there so early?

RICHARD: Sit down, Barbara.

MARIAN: Don't tell her to sit down, Richard. She
doesn't like that. Don't you know that by now?

(Then:)

BARBARA: I'm just saying why so early? Richard wasn't
supposed to even be here until—

RICHARD: I'm sorry, I could go someplace and come
back—

MARIAN: *(To* BARBARA*)* You said when Richard got
home! He's home. Here he is. We're all here. And we'll
all do this together. That's what we agreed.

BARBARA: He's furious with me.

MARIAN: He doesn't know what he's saying. You're
just the one who… *(Turns to* RICHARD*)* Beacon's the hot
community up here now. A lot of artists.

RICHARD: I've heard that.

MARIAN: What with Dia Beacon.

JANE: And the sculpture park across the river.

MARIAN: There are a couple of restaurants. A nice old
fashioned coffee shop. Like out of the sixties… *(Smiles)*
And, Barbara, what did we find out? You haven't told
Richard yet.

RICHARD: What?

BARBARA: Umm… There's someone already there who
years ago worked with Benjamin.

RICHARD: You're kidding? That's great.

BARBARA: I met her. I didn't like her.

MARIAN: She's a theater producer I think. Maybe she was something else. Anyway, so he already knows someone there. *(To* BARBARA*)* And what else? Tell Richard.

*(*BARBARA *doesn't.)*

MARIAN: There are two or three other actors in this home.

BARBARA: It's not a "home". They don't call it that.

MARIAN: And—there's going to be a "talent show" there. In a couple of weeks. Barbara's already got Benjamin rehearsing.

JANE: He rehearsed for us tonight.

MARIAN: *(Teasing* BARBARA*)* She's going to do her damnedest to make sure he wins.

JANE: Do they really have "winners"?

MARIAN: I'm teasing Barbara.

*(*BARBARA *suddenly hurries off to the kitchen.)*

(No one knows what to do.)

JANE: *(To* RICHARD*)* Do something.

RICHARD: What can I do? I can't even get her to sit down.

MARIAN: He told her—that he doesn't want to even bring her photograph with him. He's bringing pictures of all of us… Of… Just not her, he said. I think he'll forget that.

RICHARD: *(To* JANE*)* Have you seen this place?

JANE: Marian picked me up at Croton; that's as far as the trains were running. So she drove me by… It was on the way. *(Then, to* RICHARD*)* You staying the night?

RICHARD: I thought I might.

JANE: Where are you going to sleep?

RICHARD: *(Shrugs)* I thought maybe in Benjamin's room.

MARIAN: She's not going to let you do that.

(BARBARA returns, with nothing from the kitchen.)

BARBARA: He needs to be watched. I can't do that anymore.

RICHARD: No.

BARBARA: He nearly set the house on fire, didn't he? Here by himself. *(Then:)* I teach.

RICHARD: You have your own life.

MARIAN: He just lets people into the house. Doesn't he? Gives people things. When one of us isn't here.

(BARBARA sits back down.)

BARBARA: I suggested to Jane that she and Tim move up here and we'd pay her to watch Benjamin during the day.

(Then:)

RICHARD: Jane doesn't want to do that, Barbara.

(Then:)

(Lights fade.)

A History of Private Life

(A short time later. All still sitting. JANE has picked up the large books and she and MARIAN are looking through them as they eat. All are seriously eating a breakfast now.)

JANE: Tim called earlier tonight. "Last" night. It's now last night.

MARIAN: *(To RICHARD, about what JANE is going to say)* This is interesting. I don't know what it means.

RICHARD: What?

JANE: He's had his first day of rehearsal.

MARIAN: He's doing a musical. *(To* RICHARD *noticing)* You are hungry.

BARBARA: It's like lunchtime for him.

RICHARD: What show is Tim doing? He told me.

JANE: That musical. Based on that Joyce story. He's done it before.

MARIAN: Someone pulled out at the last minute.

RICHARD: He said. *(He reaches for something, and moves the wine bottle out of his way.)*

BARBARA: *(About the wine bottle)* Marian thinks Benjamin is trying to drink himself to death. We let him do what he wants now. I stopped fighting.

(Then:)

JANE: Anyway, he says the director—

BARBARA: *(To* RICHARD*)* On Tuesdays— *(Realizes)* today's Tuesday. We have chorus. Marian and… So we drop him off at Fosters. He sits and drinks and talks there. You didn't know about that.

RICHARD: Makes sense.

JANE: *(Continuing)* The director made a little speech to the actors. The director said—he wanted to be very clear about what they were trying to do.

RICHARD: What did he— *(mean)*?

JANE: He said—our job—that is, the actors' job—is to put people on the stage who are as complicated, confused, lost, ambiguous, *(Turns to* MARIAN*)* What else?

MARIAN: I didn't talk to him.

JANE: *(Continues)*—frustrated, uncertain—as any one person in the audience. *(Then:)* And then the director said—and of course we will always fail.

(Then:)

MARIAN: Interesting, isn't it?

JANE: Tim said he loved hearing that. Said it gave him goose bumps. Anyway that's what made me think of these books I had with me. And I showed Barbara and Marian—

RICHARD: *(Making a joke about how big they are, as he lifts one)* My god, they're huge! *(Pretends to "try" and lift one.)*

JANE: I found them; actually Tim did. Someone had mentioned these—an actor, of course. Said they were so useful for his research. And I was intrigued by the title.

MARIAN: *(Explaining to* RICHARD*)* We were looking through them earlier.

RICHARD: *(So heavy)* You brought these up on the train?

JANE: I know. Crazy. I thought I'd do a little light reading… *(Smiles)* Take some notes. What else is there to do in Rhinebeck? And I'm staying a week.

RICHARD: *(About his own idea)* So you already have an idea for your next book.

JANE: I don't know. The story about President Pierce was interesting too.

*(*BARBARA *suddenly stands.)*

BARBARA: I can make pancakes.

MARIAN: Barbara, we have— *(plenty)*

BARBARA: Then you don't have to have any. Richard?

RICHARD: I've already eaten…I've had eggs. There's cereal. There's mu shu.

(BARBARA *sits back down.*)

MARIAN: *(To* BARBARA*)* You want to check on him?

RICHARD: You were saying, Jane. About this idea for a book...

JANE: *(Reads the title) A History of Private Life.*

(JANE *opens one to a marked page.* MARIAN *also has one of the books.*)

JANE: We found some interesting things. This is about the middle ages: *(Reads:)* "Did people undress when they made love? The length of time that it takes the husbands in various tales to recognize their wife's true nature makes one doubt it..." What we don't know. And this— *(She reads from another marked page:)* "Even if the historian cannot hope to discover the private thoughts of people, he can identify the places where they thought and the objects on which their thoughts centered." Ordinary things. A comb. *(Shows)* A picture of a comb.

MARIAN: *(With her book open to an entry)* Jane?

JANE: Marian found something very interesting.

MARIAN: *(Reads from her book:)* "In the 19th century the battle against masturbation was waged by parents, priests, and above all—physicians. Women who rode horseback aroused their suspicions"—and here, Richard, the three of us couldn't figure this out, maybe you can help, you always seem to know things: "who rode horseback aroused their suspicions *as did the sewing machine*".

RICHARD: Maybe—

MARIAN: *(To the sisters)* I told you he'd have an opinion. I was joking, Richard. Why would I ask you—? It's the peddle. *(She demonstrates:)* They pumped a pedal.

JANE: And the vibration.

MARIAN: That too. *(To the sisters)* He was going to tell us. Unbelievable.

RICHARD: I thought you were asking—

JANE: *(Over this)* So all those photographs of women in those long rows of sweat shop workers, pumping away? You start to wonder if maybe something else was going on.

(Smiles)

MARIAN: They're still sweatshops, Jane.

JANE: Please don't take everything seriously. Jesus. It was a joke. *(Reads from a third book:)* "Increasingly private toilet facilities encouraged communion with the self. Around 1900 when bathrooms first began to be equipped with locks, it became possible for people to experience their naked bodies without fear of intrusion. The bathroom was transformed into a place for contemplation and taking stock."

RICHARD: This *is* interesting. "Taking stock."

JANE: You see why I think there might be a book here.

MARIAN: And it is sort of a follow-up, in a way, from her American Manners book.

JANE: The private life. What no one sees. What we otherwise keep hidden. Ordinary things. How they have meaning. A dinner, a bath. How one looks at oneself when alone. There's a world we don't know. And of course rarely if ever see.

(MARIAN has her book open to an entry.)

JANE: *(To MARIAN)* Do you want to read that one Marian?

MARIAN: *(Reads:)* "When suffering became too great, suicide was a possible option. More than half of all male suicides chose to hang themselves. Half of all successful female suicides chose drowning." *(Looks up, then continues:)* "Most nineteenth century suicides were committed—" Listen to this. It's not what you think. "were committed in the morning or afternoon; nighttime was seldom chosen. The rate rose from January to June, then declined from July to December. Long days, sunshine, the spectacle of people outdoors, and the beauty of nature seem to have provoked more suicides than did the solitude of evening, the chill of winter, the tortures of the night…"

(They notice BENJAMIN, *still in the same clothes, still in stocking feet, has just entered.)*

*(*BENJAMIN *smiles at them.)*

(This surprises RICHARD *who looks to his sisters.)*

JANE: What have you been doing, Uncle?

BARBARA: Not getting himself dressed. Obviously.

JANE: What have you been doing?

*(*BENJAMIN *looks at* RICHARD *and nods.)*

BARBARA: It's Richard.

BENJAMIN: I know it's Richard.

BARBARA: You said hello to him twenty minutes ago.

RICHARD: Barbara…

JANE: *(Again)* What have you been doing?

(Then:)

BENJAMIN: Writing.

MARIAN: In your journal?

RICHARD: What—?

*(*BENJAMIN *nods.)*

JANE: Good for you.

(Looks at BARBARA *and smiles)*

RICHARD: He's keeping a journal? You're keeping a journal, Uncle? *(To* MARIAN*)* That's a very good idea.

BENJAMIN: Yes.

MARIAN: Barbara's idea.

RICHARD: Why am I not surprised? *(To* BARBARA*)* And he writes in it? *(To* BENJAMIN*)* You write in it?

BENJAMIN: I do. I write in it.

(Then:)

MARIAN: Why don't you get it, Uncle?

BARBARA: Marian—

MARIAN: Richard would like to see it.

BENJAMIN: Richard?

RICHARD: I would—

BARBARA: *(Knows what she's up to)* Marian—!

JANE: Good idea.

BARBARA: Jane—

RICHARD: I'd like that.

MARIAN: *(Getting up)* Let's go and get your journal, Uncle. Come on.

BARBARA: Marian—

RICHARD: *(To* BARBARA*)* What's wrong?

*(*BENJAMIN *and* MARIAN *head off into the living room.)*

BARBARA: *(Calls)* Then also bring his shoes! They're by the T V, I think! *(To* JANE*)* Is this necessary?

RICHARD: *(Confused)* What?

BARBARA: *(Ignoring the question)* He's going to want to go out for a cigarette. And then he'll be looking for his shoes…

RICHARD: *(To* JANE*)* He doesn't appear at all upset now... Does he know what's happening? Where he's going?

JANE: No. No. *(Shrugs)* He forgets. He's forgotten...

(Then:)

(Lights fade.)

Missing Pages

(A short time later. BARBARA, JANE *and* RICHARD *still at the table)*

*(*BENJAMIN *and* MARIAN *have just returned; he holds his notebook/journal; she carries his shoes.)*

*(*BARBARA *stands up and goes to the puzzle table, to keep her distance.* RICHARD *watches this.)*

BENJAMIN: What should I read?

JANE: Give it to Richard, Uncle.

BENJAMIN: I'd rather—

MARIAN: Benjamin says he wants to read from it.

JANE: Let Richard see it, Uncle.

MARIAN: He wants to.

JANE: Barbara?

BARBARA: It's his journal.

(The siblings look at each other.)

RICHARD: Sit down.

(As BENJAMIN *sits:)*

JANE: Do you want anything?

BENJAMIN: *(To* RICHARD*)* What do you want me to read?

MARIAN: Richard doesn't know. Let me find a place...

(MARIAN *tries to hand the shoes to* BARBARA *who doesn't take them.* MARIAN *sets them down.*)

MARIAN: *(Not expecting an answer)* Barbara, anywhere you'd like to suggest?

(MARIAN *looks through the journal.* BARBARA *says nothing.* RICHARD *watches this closely.*)

MARIAN: What about...here... Start here... This is a good place.

(Pointing to a place, MARIAN *hands* BENJAMIN *back the journal.)*

(RICHARD *looks at* BARBARA.)

RICHARD: *(Concerned)* Barbara?

MARIAN: *(To* BENJAMIN*)* Go ahead...

BENJAMIN: *(Reads)* "Saturday. I am brought to an acceptance of the fact that damage has been done to my memory, and my knowledge of this has been strengthened by the realization that it is hard for me to draw conscious memories of previous events. It's important to prepare for the worst, because if you don't, you risk being in a state of denying the problem."

RICHARD: *(To* BARBARA*)* Are you all right? *(To sisters)* What's going on?

MARIAN: Read, Uncle. You stopped there... *(Points)*

BENJAMIN: *(Reads)* "I've been reading a book but I've been unable to recall actually what I've read. I need to work with a system which I can trust in the same way that I have always been able to rely on my conscious recollection to confirm that something was true."

RICHARD: When is this?

(MARIAN *shrugs.*)

BENJAMIN: "But now I need to find a new system—to find what is true. The system I am learning to rely upon involves my trusting my own writing. I must learn to look in my journal when I want to know if something is true."

JANE: You'll get a sense of what you've missed, Richard.

RICHARD: *(Confused)* What I...?

BENJAMIN: *(Reads)* "Saturday."

MARIAN: Another Saturday. Some other Saturday.

BENJAMIN: "I didn't want to get up, feeling depressed. Barbara went to the grocery store and bought fish and flowers. She helped me get up. We went for a walk at the Mills Mansion. Marian suddenly was there too. She had cookies. I told Barbara my silence was an aspect of depression." *(Another entry. Reads:)* "Wednesday. Barbara says, "Remember always to mark the date and time...""

BARBARA: I can never get him to put in the dates. *(Shrugs)* So it all runs together...

MARIAN: *(Over this)* Let him read, Barbara...

BENJAMIN: "Barbara takes me to see a play called *The Death Of A Salesman.*"

BARBARA: He knew the director.

MARIAN: Last spring.

BENJAMIN: "I must not forget that we went to the theater by subway, the first time I've undertaken such a journey since my illness began." *(Turns page)* "I must recover from the rather blank depressed tone of these pages. What is the matter with me? I don't feel that all the time, it's true, but much too often for comfort."

RICHARD: It's like we're listening to him talk to himself.

(BENJAMIN *hears this and looks at* RICHARD.)

MARIAN: *(To* RICHARD*)* Just listen. Uncle…?

BENJAMIN: This page is torn out.

RICHARD: What do you mean?

BENJAMIN: *(Noticing)* Another page torn out…

(RICHARD *looks to* MARIAN *then to* JANE.)

BENJAMIN: "Saw a film in Italian at Upstate with Barbara tonight. She says I am now a member. It's Barbara's birthday."

MARIAN: *(Stating the obvious, they all know when Barbara's birthday is)* Four months ago.

BENJAMIN: "I have realized that losing my memory has always been a source of fear, but I must cope with it. And now—look! I'm coping with it." *(He looks up and smiles, even laughs as he thinks that's funny. Then notices:)* Another page torn out. Another. Another.

RICHARD: *(Confused)* Marian—?

JANE: Sh-sh…

(Then:)

BENJAMIN: "Someone came to dinner. We sat on the porch for a while so I could smoke. I felt very tired though because there was a mishap over the medicine. Barbara is driving me mad, continually reminding me to 'write what I feel'."

(RICHARD *looks at* BARBARA, BENJAMIN *turns a page.*)

BENJAMIN: "Wednesday. Barbara and I looked at my journal together. We looked at the entry for Saturday and saw I had written: 'Barbara is driving me mad, continually reminding me to write what I feel' I feel upset. But I could see she was right. I ask her: why are you tearing out pages in my journal?" *(He looks at* BARBARA. *New entry:) (Reads)* "Watching a video at Lincoln Center. Barbara and I watch together."

BARBARA: I took you to the library there. They have shows on video.

MARIAN: *(Over)* Barbara.

BARBARA: *(Continuing)* They have *The Cherry Orchard* you were in at BAM. Your Gaev.

BENJAMIN: *(Reads)* "I don't recognize myself."

BARBARA: *(To* BENJAMIN*)* In the video. *(Without looking at the journal)* You wrote this on the train home.

MARIAN: *(Over)* Barbara, please.

BARBARA: That's why your handwriting's... The ride was bumpy.

(BENJAMIN *turns a page.)*

BENJAMIN: *(Reads)* "9:55 P M. Pitch dark outside. That's all I want to write." *(Turns the page.)* "I walk back from the bank on my own. And later to the bookshop where I meet Barbara. We had coffee and Barbara was very fetching. I stand among all the books and look at her a long time. *(Next: Reads:)* "Barbara has just torn a page out of my journal..." *(He looks up. To* BARBARA*)* That's what it says. That's what's written.

BARBARA: I know.

BENJAMIN: "... has just torn a page out of my journal. I ask Barbara to give the page back to me. She does. I copy it back into my journal. Here it is, I quote: "Today I stare at Barbara in the shower. She does not see me. I stand in the door and watch her for a long time. She's—so... " *(Looks up, to* BARBARA*)*

BARBARA: *(To* BENJAMIN*)* I scratched that word out. I scribbled over it.

(BENJAMIN *nods.)*

BENJAMIN: *(Reads)* "She's so—" something, whatever
"… and—beautiful…Barbara won't let me copy
down any more of the page. Barbara sits with me
on the couch and cries. I ask Barbara what I was like
before…"

BARBARA: *(Standing)* That's enough… *(She takes the
journal and closes it.)*

(Pause)

*(*BENJAMIN *stands.)*

BARBARA: Do you want a cigarette, Benjamin? You
need to put on your shoes first.

BENJAMIN: *(To* BARBARA*)* I can put my shoes on.

*(*BARBARA *helps* BENJAMIN*.)*

BARBARA: I know you can. It's just a little easier… With
help.

(Awkward pause, as BARBARA *gets on* BENJAMIN'*s shoes.)*

BENJAMIN: *(Frustrated)* I can do it!

BARBARA: Do you have your cigarettes?

*(*BENJAMIN *shows* BARBARA*.)*

BARBARA: Stay in the backyard.

*(*BENJAMIN *goes off into the kitchen to go outside.)*

(Short pause)

RICHARD: What did he write—in the pages you ripped
out?

MARIAN: *(Answering for* BARBARA*)* Different things.
One night he came down to the basement where
Barbara sleeps, and just watched her. *(Then:)* For god
knows how long. He wrote about that. He described
that. Barbara hid this for months. It's been going on
for months. Since long before you went to England,
Richard. Then it just came out. *(Then:)* We talked to

his therapist. Barbara showed her some of the pages.
I made her do that. I think she even showed the
therapist pages she won't show me. Is that right?

(No answer)

MARIAN: There are pages she won't show me. I was
scared. What is going on in that head of his? We have
no idea.

BARBARA: We have some idea... *(Laughs to herself)*

RICHARD: What did the therapist say? *(Realizing, to*
JANE, *"of course")* You know all about this...

(JANE nods.)

MARIAN: *(Defensive)* You were away.

JANE: *(To* BARBARA*)* Barbara, tell Richard about...

(BARBARA turns away.)

JANE: *(To* BARBARA*)* He needs to know. He's our
brother. *(To* RICHARD*)* One of the younger teachers
came over. Had to talk to Barbara about something.
Right? Marian told me this. Not Barbara. A very
attractive young woman. Teaches chemistry? Barbara
walks in and Benjamin's talking to her. He's telling her
that she has two very nice firm lovely breasts. Could he
touch them? *(To* BARBARA*)* The poor woman was beet
red? *(Then:)* Could he "rub them"?

MARIAN: I asked the therapist if she felt—could he ever
do more than just talk? She said—she didn't know.
Maybe. Maybe. So be on our guard.

(Short pause)

RICHARD: Has he? *(Then:)* Has he tried to do more than
just talk, Barbara?

(Short pause)

MARIAN: I don't know.

(MARIAN looks at at BARBARA who says nothing.)

RICHARD: I'm sorry, Barbara. This is…

(Then:)

BARBARA: I still think I can handle this.

MARIAN: You agreed—

BARBARA: *(To* MARIAN*)* I know I agreed! You made me agree! But I think he's gotten better. Richard saw him tonight. What did you think, Richard?

RICHARD: Barbara—

BARBARA: You saw him tell stories. Remember things.

*(*RICHARD *Says nothing.)*

*(*BARBARA *stands and heads for the kitchen.)*

MARIAN: *("Looks" at her watch as she "calmly":)* We'll be leaving in a few hours, Barbara.

BARBARA: Fuck you Marian!!! *(She hurries off to the kitchen.)*

MARIAN: *(To* RICHARD, *but loud enough for* BARBARA *to hear)* He's already packed. *(Shouts)* She agreed!

RICHARD: Marian—

*(*BARBARA *hurries back, she never made it to the kitchen, this isn't over:)*

BARBARA: Richard's here, why can't we ask him?! Why is he here then?!

MARIAN: Ask him.

*(*BARBARA *and* MARIAN *look to* RICHARD.*)*

RICHARD: What??

(Spent, BARBARA *has gone off into the kitchen.)*

MARIAN: You're just being selfish! And you know that!

RICHARD: Marian—

MARIAN: *(Shouts to* BARBARA*)* Grow up!! *(Then: "smiling" to* RICHARD*)* And she's the oldest…

(Pause)

JANE: *(To* RICHARD*)* The therapist— *(Looks for the word)*
—"thinks" that because of the memory loss, there's
also the loss of inhibitions. That what's going on. And
it's just going to get worse.

(Then:)

MARIAN: *(To* RICHARD*)* This is hard for her. For all of
us, of course, but… We have a few hours. The sun's not
even up yet. *(Stands)* Are we finished?

RICHARD: *(Stopping her)* I'm not.

*(*MARIAN *sits back down.)*

RICHARD: I'm going to have a drink.

*(*JANE *looks at* RICHARD*.)*

RICHARD: It's like almost noon—in England. *(Pours
himself a glass of water in his juice glass, swirls it around to
clean it, then drinks, then pours wine into the now "clean"
glass.)*

*(*JANE *watches* RICHARD *do this.)*

MARIAN: So how was London? You haven't said
anything.

RICHARD: Nothing much to say. I took depositions.

JANE: *(About rinsing the glass, etc)* Have you cleaned a
glass like that before?

RICHARD: In college. But with beer.

(No one knows what to say.)

JANE: I never go anywhere.

MARIAN: *(Looking off toward the kitchen)* You're going to
Chicago for Thanksgiving.

JANE: By bus…

*(*MARIAN *gets up and goes to the kitchen.)*

(They watch her go. Then:)

RICHARD: Did you know about--?

JANE: They keep secrets those two. You must know that by now. Marian made Barbara tell me when I got here on Friday. They showed me the journal... *(Then:)* There's more that she didn't rip out...

RICHARD: I think we do what Barbara wants us to do. She's been the one—

JANE: She keeps changing her mind, Richard.

RICHARD: *(Sighs then)* Has Benjamin really forgotten about today? That he's going? What's happening?

JANE: *(Shrugs)* Seems like it.

RICHARD: And they're not going to remind him?

JANE: I get that impression, don't you?

RICHARD: And we're not going to? Is that right? The right thing for us to do?

JANE: I don't know. I don't know. *(Then)* You tell him then.

(Then:)

RICHARD: *(New thought)* Tim okay?

JANE: He's great.

(MARIAN returns without BARBARA.)

MARIAN: She's doing dishes. She'll be okay. You know Barbara, now she's embarrassed. *(Goes to the puzzle)*

JANE: *(To RICHARD)* Can I have a sip? *(She sips from RICHARD's glass.)*

MARIAN: *(At the puzzle)* Should we get clean glasses? Why not? *(Starts to go)*

JANE: These are fine. We're family...

(Lights fade.)

Firs

(A moment later, RICHARD talking about England, as they all drink, and pick at the food. Perhaps even the Chinese food now.)

RICHARD: An old friend was passing through London.

(BARBARA has just arrived in the door way. RICHARD looks at BARBARA.)

RICHARD: They were asking me about London, Barbara. *(Back to JANE and MARIAN)* An old friend was passing through London. We'd been together at the Attorney General's office. For both Eliot and Cuomo. He's still quite close to Andrew.

(MARIAN gestures for BARBARA to come and sit with her by the puzzle. It will take her some time, but she will go and sit with MARIAN.)

RICHARD: And they'd had a dinner together, he said, where my name came up two three times. Andrew himself brought it up. He said I was an example of a lawyer who was totally fair. Who didn't carry any—"agenda". By which I think Andrew meant—I don't "believe in anything".

(RICHARD smiles. The sisters don't.)

RICHARD: And that I was, he said, just the sort they now needed up in Albany. I'm guessing my friend was told to tell me that.

JANE: You hate Andrew Cuomo, Richard. You make fun of him. You don't trust him.

RICHARD: That's true. I don't—

JANE: *(Obvious)* "The Dark Prince."

MARIAN: He's done some good things—. Hasn't he?

RICHARD: *(Over this)* Maybe what we need right now is— "ruthless". God knows he's that. Anyway... *He* knows how to lead. We'd know who he was.

MARIAN: Richard—

RICHARD: The question of course is—where he'd lead us.

MARIAN: That's what I was going to say—

JANE: *(Over the end of this)* He's in it for himself.

RICHARD: And that's—unique? If you eliminate all politicians who--

JANE: You're not seriously considering...

BARBARA: *(To MARIAN)* He's sitting in the backyard. I left him alone.

(They eat. JANE looks at her sisters.)

RICHARD: *(Eating)* Andrew's pumping money into Buffalo. So he can be the governor who "turned around" a rust-belt city. That plays well in—Ohio. Michigan... He's always thinking...

JANE: About whom?

(Pause)

RICHARD: This same friend? We got together three, four times. I think we were both just lonely. One night we went to see a show. A character in the play talks about visiting the men's public bathroom in some fancy part of London years and years ago. The walls are all marble. And the urinals have glass tanks full of water. In each tank swam ten, maybe twenty gold fish. And so—you'd flush and suddenly the water level would go down, and he said the fish would huddle together and you could see a real 'consternation' on their faces. *(Then:)* But then—the water would start to fill up again, and so would rise, and the fish, he said, they all relaxed—because everything was going to be fine after all. And then—someone would flush again… *(Smiles)* My friend leaned over and said, "That's how it is going to be like on election night." Hope…and change… *(Then:)* Glad I'm not in the city tonight…God, what that'll be like. *(Then:)* Speaking of England. I got presents for you. They're in the car. *(He gets up.)*

JANE: We weren't expecting—

RICHARD: I'll get the gifts. *(He goes.)*

JANE: Shouldn't we get dressed?

MARIAN: *(To* BARBARA*)* Are you going to vote before we go to Beacon? Or when we come back? I suppose when we come back, it'll be something for you to do.

BARBARA: I don't need something to do.

MARIAN: To take your mind— *(Stops herself)*

(Then:)

JANE: *(To no one)* I'm not registered here.

MARIAN: *(To* BARBARA*)* I thought I would vote. Polls are open. They open at six.

JANE: Why are we not surprised?

*(*JANE *smiles to* BARBARA. BARBARA *at the puzzle smiles to herself.)*

MARIAN: What? Why are you smiling? I want to vote. It's not what you both think. Jesus.

JANE: *(Changing the subject, to* BARBARA*)* I think Richard wants to quit his job. All that about Cuomo… What do you think, Barbara?

BARBARA: Pamela wouldn't be too happy. *(Shrugs)* I don't know. He's got kids. He's just talking. We just talk.

MARIAN: I don't think he's saved anything. He seems to spend what he makes. I'm guessing, that he feels ashamed about the work he's doing-so he hasn't really earned it.

JANE: *(To no one)* Or he just likes to spend money...

(JANE sees BENJAMIN coming:)

JANE: Benjamin.

BARBARA: *(Getting up)* Benjamin! Why don't you sit here, work on the puzzle. It's too hard for me. I need your help.

(RICHARD enters with a shopping bag.)

RICHARD: *(To BENJAMIN)* There you are. *(To his sisters)* He was sitting on the front steps. I said he should come in.

(BENJAMIN goes to BARBARA's chair, she brings another chair to the table.)

JANE: *(About the shopping bag)* Richard, you really didn't need to— We don't expect gifts.

MARIAN: I do. I'm joking.

JANE: She's not.

BARBARA: *(Over this, to BENJAMIN about the puzzle)* I was trying to work on the tablecloth—the white there...

(BENJAMIN looks and smiles at BARBARA.)

(The others notices this.)

RICHARD: *(While watching)* I wanted to, Jane. It gave me a reason to get out of the hotel room.

MARIAN: Uncle, Richard's bought us presents.

RICHARD: *(Realizing)* I didn't bring anything for— (Benjamin). I should have. I don't know why I didn't think—

BARBARA: You should have, Richard. You should have thought of that. What's wrong with you?

(Then:)

RICHARD: Sorry. *(He opens the bag—presents wrapped in Christmas wrapping. then, handing out the gifts:)* Jane. Marian. Pamela only had Christmas wrapping… Barbara.

(They are not well wrapped.)

JANE: You wrapped them yourself. *(To her sisters)* That's cute.

RICHARD: How could you tell?

(JANE and MARIAN share a look.)

MARIAN: *(As she and JANE open their gifts)* Pamela let you wrap these yourself? *(To JANE)* That's very unlike her.

RICHARD: She was asleep.

(BARBARA hasn't begun to open hers.)

(RICHARD watches as she does the puzzle:)

RICHARD: I didn't get you anything Uncle. I always think of you as the man who has everything.

BENJAMIN: *(In a smiling happy mood now)* I do!

(BENJAMIN reaches across the card table and surprises BARBARA by taking her hand. He holds it.)

(The others try not to watch, as BENJAMIN kisses her hand. She lets him, "smiles" at him, then she takes her hand back To "open" the present:)

BARBARA: *(To BENJAMIN, explaining as she removes her hand)* I have to open my present.

JANE: *(Changing the subject, having opened her gift—a sweater. She holds it up)* It's beautiful, Richard. Is it cashmere? You shouldn't have—

MARIAN: *(Her point earlier)* He likes to spend his money.

RICHARD: *(Oblivious)* I do. That's true. *(Laughs. To*
BARBARA *and* MARIAN, *who have opened their presents:)* I
got both of you the same scarf.

BARBARA: It's very pretty, Richard. Isn't it, Benjamin?

RICHARD: *(Explaining the same gift, over this)* Remember
the last time—and you two argued over—. I thought
this would be easier. The same scarf.

(No one is listening to RICHARD.*)*

MARIAN: *(To* BARBARA*)* They must have cost—

BARBARA: Handmade. *(Looks to the label)* From—.
(Decides not to read the label) Handmade. Thank you,
Richard.

*(*BARBARA *kisses* RICHARD *on the cheek.)*

RICHARD: *(A joke)* I didn't want you two fighting over—

MARIAN: *(Thanking him)* How much did they—?

BARBARA: Marian, don't ask. He can't take them back...

RICHARD: You don't like them?

BARBARA: *(No enthusiasm)* We—love them. We love
them. Here... *(She puts her scarf around* BENJAMIN*'s*
shoulders.) Like an ascot. Didn't he used to wear—?

JANE: I think you did, Benjamin—

BARBARA: I remember. When we were kids. *(She looks at*
BENJAMIN, *smiles at him.)* I have a picture somewhere...

MARIAN: *(Distracting her)* We were just saying, we
should get dressed. Barbara? *(To* BARBARA*)* Come on.
We should get dressed.

BARBARA: We're not going for a few hours.

MARIAN: *(Over this)* We should get dressed.

BENJAMIN: *(At the puzzle)* Are we going somewhere?
(This stops the room.)

(JANE *has put her sweater on over her nightgown.*)

JANE: (*Then*) They're going to vote, Uncle. It's election day. (*As a joke*) Who are you voting for?

BENJAMIN: (*At the puzzle*) I don't know.

BARBARA: (*Staring at* BENJAMIN) He used to wear the ascot when he took us out to dinner. When Dad wasn't around... He'd take Mom and us out to dinner... My god...

JANE: What?

BARBARA: It's just sparked so many memories.

MARIAN: (*To* BARBARA) Come on. Come on.

RICHARD: Barbara. I was thinking when I was outside just now. That— (*He looks at* BENJAMIN, *then:*) —and I need to choose my words carefully—that all of this, what we're doing, what we have to do, I know it's hard. For you especially. Actually I can't imagine how hard it must be.

BENJAMIN: What?

JANE: Nothing, Uncle.

RICHARD: But—I really do think it will help you get on with your life.

BARBARA: Go to hell, Richard.

(BARBARA *goes,* MARIAN *right behind her.*)

RICHARD: What?

MARIAN: (*As they go*) He means well...

BENJAMIN: (*Laughs to* RICHARD) I've never heard Barbara say that before to anyone...

JANE: (*Calls*) I'll pick up!

MARIAN: (*Off*) Get Richard to help!

RICHARD: I meant –

JANE: I know what you meant. What did you expect her to say? Thank you? *(She starts to pick up things.)*

RICHARD: I can help.

JANE: Yes, Richard. You can help.

RICHARD: What did I say?

(No response, then:)

RICHARD: *(About* BARBARA *and* BENJAMIN*)* I had no idea about all she's been going through.

JANE: She thought she could handle it. Barbara always thinks that. She only told Marian when Marian happened to read the book *(Gestures: "Benjamin's journal")* with him and—

RICHARD: *(Looking at* BENJAMIN*)* He hasn't done—?

JANE: Barbara would have told us that. *(Then:)* But I'm sure there are "incidents" —like the watching, that she hasn't told us. She's scared.

BENJAMIN: What are you talking about?

JANE: *(To make a point to* RICHARD*)* Uncle, I hear that you sometimes call Barbara— "Laura".

RICHARD: Really?

BENJAMIN: *(Same time)* Do I?

JANE: That was our Mother's name. *(To* RICHARD*)* Barbara sort of looks like her.

RICHARD: She does. A little.

JANE: So I can see how one could get confused.

BENJAMIN: Did I know your mother?

JANE: Yes, you did, Benjamin. You knew her very very well. *(Then: To* RICHARD*)* Don't expect Barbara to appreciate that you think she's been wasting her life doing this— *(Gestures to* BENJAMIN*)*

RICHARD: Is that what she heard?

JANE: We'll pick up later. We've got time. *(She sits at the table.)* You can sometimes be so goddamn thick. I'm hungry... *(She looks in the Chinese food.)* Sit down... Have an egg roll...

RICHARD: *(About* BARBARA*)* That's not what I meant—

JANE: I know. And she probably knows it too. Sit down. *(Then:)* We've been waiting for you. *(Looks at him)* Are you thinking of quitting your job? That's what all that sounded like to me.

(No response)

JANE: Tim thinks we should move to Rhinebeck.

RICHARD: I know. It's a nice place.

JANE: Pour me a drink.

*(*RICHARD *pours.)*

JANE: Tim says he wants to raise a pig for the Dutchess County Fair.

RICHARD: You're kidding.

JANE: He says he thinks it must be like doing a play. Because there's a beginning, middle and end...

*(*JANE *and* RICHARD *smile.)*

JANE: The strangest things come out of his mouth. Actors...

RICHARD: What do you want?

JANE: There are restaurants here. He could get a waiter job I think in a heartbeat. Having experience in New York. *(Then answering his question:)* I'm thinking about it too.

RICHARD: Do you know yet when—or if—they'll bring your book out?

(Short pause)

JANE: I took it away from them. They were taking their time. *(Then:)* I'm going to start a new book.

RICHARD: I know. We were just talking about what that could—

JANE: *(Changing the subject)* Tim wants to have his daughter full time—

RICHARD: I heard.

JANE: Karen's a very sweet girl. Marian falls all over her.

RICHARD: Why does that not surprise me.

JANE: You know Marian now has a girl scout troop?

RICHARD: No. I didn't know…

(BARBARA returns dressed now.)

RICHARD: Barbara, I'm sorry—

BARBARA: I thought you were picking up—

JANE: Sit down. And join us. Let's live in a mess for a change.

BARBARA: For a change?

JANE: I mean—in terms of dirty dishes.

RICHARD: Have a glass of wine, Barbara.

(BARBARA looks at BENJAMIN.)

RICHARD: He's been working hard on that puzzle. Really concentrating.

(BARBARA begins to pick up.)

JANE: *(To "RICHARD")* Marian was telling me about Barbara and her dish washing? Marian said no matter how well she did the dishes—how much she cleaned up and scrubbed everything, Barbara always finds one thing more to do. She has to do the last thing.

(BARBARA takes some dirty dishes out into the kitchen.)

JANE: A glass, a spot on the counter. This drove Marian crazy for a while, then she decided that she'd always leave one thing unfinished. So Barbara can do that. She said she feels like one of the Muslim rug-makers who leave one fault in the rug on purpose as their homage to Allah.

(BARBARA *has returned with a tray and continues to straighten up.)*

JANE: *(To* RICHARD*)* Marian has a boyfriend. Barbara told me. *(To* BARBARA*)* When you said that was a secret, you didn't' mean from Richard, did you?

BARBARA: *(To* JANE*)* That sweater will look better when you're not in your nightgown.

JANE: I'm getting dressed. *(Makes a face at* RICHARD *about* BARBARA. *To* BARBARA:*)* You don't have to tell me to get dressed. *(Then: To* RICHARD*)* Marian's new boyfriend is poll watching now. That's why she can't wait to vote.

BARBARA: *(Getting up)* What about dessert, Richard?

JANE: He just had breakfast.

BARBARA: He's been eating Chinese food. *I* feel like dessert. *(She starts to go.)* You all right there, Uncle? *(She goes with the tray of dirty dishes.)*

JANE: *(To* BENJAMIN*)* You find a piece that fits yet?

BENJAMIN: Not yet.

JANE: You know you can't force them. *(Then: to* RICHARD*)* Barbara's a little jealous I think. About Marian's boyfriend.

RICHARD: I doubt that. If she didn't want you to tell me, then— *(To change the subject:)* I haven't asked you how Billy is.

JANE: Got a job. Part time. Which he sort of likes. That's not easy for kids these days.

RICHARD: No. It isn't easy.

(BARBARA *returns with ice cream, plates, etc.*)

BARBARA: What "isn't"?

JANE: Billy.

BARBARA: Oh. Yes. Good for him. Tell Richard about Billy and the intern. Who wants that disgusting fake whipped cream that Marian bought? (*Then:*) I think I do. (*As she heads off:*)

RICHARD: Barbara is there another bottle of wine? (*Then:*) What intern?

JANE: At Billy's job—. An intern arrives. She arrives *with* another young woman. Who's that, everyone's wondering. Then the intern introduces the woman as "my personal assistant".

RICHARD: You're kidding.

(MARIAN *enters, now dressed.*)

JANE: (*To* MARIAN) The intern.

MARIAN: Oh god.

JANE: She started her day by giving dictation to her assistant. "If you need anything and I'm not around," she told everyone, "just ask my personal assistant".

(*To* MARIAN *who stands over* BENJAMIN *at the puzzle.*)

JANE: Barbara's getting dessert.

MARIAN: Good. (*Picks up a puzzle piece.*) I hope it's chocolate—something.

RICHARD: Was she handicapped in some way? The intern.

JANE: No. Just rich.

MARIAN: How's the puzzle going, Uncle? We bought that for him. (*To* BENJAMIN) You picked it out, remember? At Stickles. You said you liked it because they all seemed to be having such a nice meal together.

(BARBARA is returning with wine bottle, fake whipped cream, chocolate sauce.)

BARBARA: *(To MARIAN)* You're dressed… *(A look at JANE)*

JANE: I'm getting dressed….

BARBARA: *(Holds up bottle)* It's a screw-top, Richard. *(To MARIAN, knowing she'll ask)* I got the chocolate sauce. *(To RICHARD)* You going to want more cereal?

RICHARD: I'm switching to chocolate sauce and ice cream.

(The sisters serve themselves ice cream.)

So Marian, I hear you have a boyfriend.

MARIAN: *(Turns to BARBARA)* I said that was a secret.

BARBARA: I didn't tell him.

RICHARD: That's—good. That you do.

BARBARA: We don't think it's serious.

MARIAN: How do you know? *(To RICHARD)* We tell each other it's not serious. He's only been separated from his wife for a few months…I only met him after—

BARBARA: You've known him for years. He's lived here for years.

MARIAN: I meant… You know what I meant.

BARBARA: *(Serving the ice cream)* He's a Republican.

MARIAN: He's not a Republican. *(To RICHARD)* He's an Independent. Libertarian. Like a lot of people were in the sixties, seventies.

BARBARA: He had a Ron Paul bumper sticker on his car.

MARIAN: *(Over the end of this)* I made him take that off.

RICHARD: And you used to give me so much shit just for working with Republicans. And now she's—

(BARBARA *stands to reach for something across the table.*)

MARIAN: He's not a Republican. (*Then:*) Anyway, you see people differently, when you sleep with them.

(MARIAN *smiles,* JANE *and* RICHARD *laugh;* BARBARA *"laughs". Then:*)

JANE: That's true—when I first met Tim, I thought—

BARBARA: (*Surprised, to* MARIAN) You sleep with him??

MARIAN: (*To* BARBARA) Sit down. Sit down.

RICHARD: That's not how to get her to—

(BARBARA *sits.*)

BARBARA: (*To* MARIAN) You've only been dating him for…

MARIAN: I don't tell you everything. Because you can't keep a secret.

BARBARA: I can keep a secret.

(BARBARA *looks to* JANE *who looks down at her ice cream.*)

BARBARA: They're your brother and sister. They worry about you.

(*They eat.* RICHARD *checks his watch.* BARBARA *notices this.*)

RICHARD: So Jane was telling me Billy's doing fine in Philadelphia.

MARIAN: I visited him there.

RICHARD: Did you? Good for you. You're a good aunt. I feel like a bad Uncle.

BARBARA: It's not a competition, Richard.

(*Then:*)

MARIAN: John wanted to see a show in the museum in Philly.

RICHARD: John?

BARBARA: The boyfriend. He's a painter. Not houses. People. More money in houses. At least up here. This isn't Chelsea. Or Hudson.

MARIAN: So we went and took Billy out to lunch.

RICHARD: He can make a living painting?

MARIAN: Not a great one, but… And he has to do some teaching, which he hates. Says the students now are like "consumers". *(Then:)* I hardly knew him, and then one day out of the blue he asks me to pose for a portrait. *(To* BARBARA*) With* my clothes on. That's the first thing she asked.

BARBARA: *(Eating)* Sounds like they didn't stay on long.

MARIAN: He first asked Barbara. She was scared.

BARBARA: I wasn't "scared". We were—are—taking care of Benjamin. *(To the others)* I thought that's what we were doing.

(They look at BENJAMIN.*)*

JANE: I think he's asleep. He's bored listening to us complain. I can only imagine what we sound like sometimes…

*(*BARBARA *has stood, goes to check on* BENJAMIN.*)*

MARIAN: Let him sleep.

*(*BARBARA *nods.)*

MARIAN: He's been up all night.

JANE: So have we…

BARBARA: *(To* BENJAMIN*)* Do you want to lie down?

BENJAMIN: No.

(BARBARA *takes a cushion off of one of the chairs—*
BENJAMIN'*s chair at the table and goes to* BENJAMIN.
BARBARA *Puts the pillow on the card table, and slowly helps*
BENJAMIN'*s head onto the table.)*

RICHARD: Shouldn't he go to bed?

MARIAN: He'd just wake up. I think he likes the voices.

(BARBARA *returns to the table.)*

BARBARA: Maybe we should keep our voices down.
(Then: Quietly) I'm glad you have a "boyfriend",
Marian. She thinks I'm jealous.

MARIAN: *(To* RICHARD*)* Jane's worried about Tim—

JANE: Marian.

MARIAN: She was telling us tonight, right? That maybe
Tim has never really forgiven her for—for when she
went back to Alfred that time.

JANE: *(To* MARIAN*)* That was a secret too.

MARIAN: We told her to talk to you, Richard. How you
dealt with—when Pamela—left you. You've forgiven
her, right?

RICHARD: I've forgiven her. I haven't forgotten. But I
think I've forgiven. But you can't forget...

MARIAN: Unless you're Benjamin.

(They eat.)

MARIAN: *(Prodding* JANE *to tell more)* And Tim is right
now staying—where? With whom? Tell Richard.

JANE: He's in Chicago, staying on a friend's couch.
(To MARIAN*)* To save money. *(To* RICHARD*)* To get the
job he had to lie and say he was local. She's an old
girlfriend. Her couch. He didn't exactly tell me that at
first. When he suggested it as a "cheap alternative" to a
rented room somewhere. *(She shrugs.)*

MARIAN: *(To* RICHARD*)* So Jane thinks if she can get Tim to move to Rhinebeck—that'll sort all this out.

RICHARD: I thought it was Tim who wanted to…

(Then:)

JANE: Tim told me he went on a "pilgrimage" to Obama's pizzeria.

RICHARD: What? What's that?

JANE: In Chicago. On the South Side. Hyde Park. They had pictures of Obama all over its walls he said.

MARIAN: He went all that way—?

RICHARD: He's in Chicago.

MARIAN: I know.

JANE: The theater's around the corner.

RICHARD: Oh.

JANE: A couple of blocks away. *(Then)* Tim said he happened to go in. He wanted pizza. He was sitting there and saw all the photos. *(Then)* I guess it wasn't really a "pilgrimage".

MARIAN: *(Then, to* JANE*)* Rhinebeck's not all you and Tim might think it is.

JANE: What do you--?

BARBARA: Marian's right, Jane.

MARIAN: Look what Barbara's been going through.

RICHARD: *(Eating)* What, Barbara?

JANE: You told me. *(To* RICHARD*)* They told me.

MARIAN: You haven't told Richard? It's all been really silly. You want to tell him?

(She doesn't. She eats.)

MARIAN: There's a writer who lives around the corner on South Street. He writes novels. He wrote a novel about of all people Benedict Arnold. Barbara knows the writer, and now for years she's asked him to come into her class and the students read the book and… It's a chance for the kids to hear from a real writer. About— what? Fiction versus history? Opens up a lot of good discussion, right?

BARBARA: *(Eating)* The difference between what a novelist is after, and say a biographer—

RICHARD: *(To* BARBARA*)* I want to take your class. It always sounds so interesting.

MARIAN: In this novel, George Washington is shown to be— *(Looks to* BARBARA*)* —frustrated? Even bitter? He's even drinking a bit.

*(*RICHARD *"toasts" Washington.)*

MARIAN: Angry at the politicians.

*(*RICHARD *toasts again.)*

MARIAN: *(To* BARBARA*)* Tell him.

BARBARA: Last Friday before my friend is to come to our class—the principal wants to see me. He's in his office with the superintendent, and some parent has complained about the way Washington is treated in this novel. And now I'm told my students aren't allowed to read or discuss this book anymore. *(Then:)* I made up some excuse to the writer. I was embarrassed.

MARIAN: *(To* JANE*)* It's not the liberal haven you think it is, Jane. I keep telling her that. It's more complicated than that. Rhinebeck is not going to solve all your problems.

*(*BARBARA *smiles.)*

BARBARA: *(Eating)* Marian and I sometimes say we should move back to the city. Or into the city, she's never lived there. "Back" for me.

RICHARD: Are you serious?

BARBARA: Sell this house, quit our jobs and—to New York! To New York!

(Smiles to herself)

JANE: For what you'd get for this, maybe you could buy a closet in Queens. You never go *back* to New York. Tim and I have talked about that. We know that. You go—you go. You're gone…

MARIAN: Still, I'd like to stop teaching.

BARBARA: Marian says that all the time.

MARIAN: *(Over this)* I meant it. More and more. You used to be able to do what you thought was best. If you did good teaching, if you were passionate and energetic, kids would learn, and that would be enough. But the faith—that's the word, the "faith" we once had in ourselves—as professional teachers—. It's been ruined. By all the rankings…those tests. The… At staff meetings, right Barbara, we talk about "brain games", healthy "brain" food. No homework the week before the tests. So they can rest their little brains. *(Then:)* The really sad thing is that you now see young teachers— *(To* BARBARA*)* Correct?

BARBARA: Right.

MARIAN: We comment on this all the time. The young ones—and *this* is all they know. They think—this is what teaching is…

(Short pause. BENJAMIN, *his head on the puzzle. They look at him.* BARBARA *has gotten up and goes to* BENJAMIN.*)*

JANE: He's going to be all right there, Barbara. It's for the best. It really is.

(Then:)

MARIAN: Are we doing the right thing, Richard? We waited for you to come home to tell us. *(Then: Quietly)* Barbara…

(BARBARA *looks at* BENJAMIN.)

BARBARA: *(Whispers to the others)* What it must feel
like… All the things you feel you're missing… The
gaps… My god… *(To* JANE*)* Talk about a private life…

(They watch BENJAMIN, *then:)*

MARIAN: I was listening in the car the other day to
N P R. They were talking about that feeling—of
missing something. The worry of having missed that
day of 'school' when they talked about something that
everyone else now knows—but you.

BARBARA: That's what he must feel about everything.
Every day.

MARIAN: They talked about a woman, a friend of one
of theirs—a smart woman, maybe thirty years old, with
a good job. One day, she's on a committee for a benefit,
I think, and it's been decided that there would be a
petting zoo, at the benefit. So they go around the table,
someone suggests: sheep. Another a horse. A third: he
knows someone who has a llama. And then it's this
woman's turn and she says: how about a unicorn?
(Then:) Everyone thinks she's joking. They laugh. But
it's soon clear that she's not. Somehow in her thirty
some years, which included a very good and expensive
education, she's missed the fact that unicorns weren't
real. *(Laughs)* She said it made her wonder: what else
has she missed? What else doesn't she know that
everyone else does?

(BARBARA *has sat with* BENJAMIN *at the puzzle table.)*

RICHARD: Or you make "leaps" trying to make sense
of things that at first don't make sense. It must be—
"wired" into us—this need to try and make sense of
things.

BARBARA: What do you mean?

RICHARD: When I got the flu in London?

MARIAN: You got the flu?

JANE: And did he whine about that. In his emails.

MARIAN: *(To* BARBARA*)* Did you know he had the flu?

(BARBARA *shakes her head.)*

MARIAN: How come you tell Jane--?

JANE: *(Shushing her)* Marian—

RICHARD: *(Over this)* I was on the couch in the hotel
room watching T V, the news. Half asleep. *(To* JANE*)*
Feeling sorry for myself. Feeling like shit. And I hear
this report on T V about a disease infecting British
sheep. And how they've just learned that the disease is
being transmitted to England from the Continent—by
midgets.

JANE: What??

RICHARD: By midgets. I'm lying there thinking, this is
odd. What a different culture this is, we may speak the
same language, but…I mean in America, we wouldn't
even use that word. Would we? I fall back asleep,
wake up, T V is still on, the news again. Same thing.
From the Continent—by midgets. Wow. I start to use
this as a way of really understanding England—its
culture; its whatever. And how different they are
from…I even start theorizing—why "midgets" and
not—other people as carriers. I'm thinking this is very
very interesting. *(Then:)* In the morning, the newspaper
is delivered to my door, and I see the same story about
the sheep. And as I read it, I suddenly see that it's not
"midgets", it's "midges" —little flies that the wind
carries…

(The sisters laugh.)

RICHARD: I'd made up this whole complicated theory…

(They look at BENJAMIN.*)*

BARBARA: This semester, I assigned my students to write a story based on Greek myths. So I decided to write one myself.

RICHARD: You're writing Barbara...

BARBARA: I write when Benjamin is writing in his journal. It helps him, I think seeing me sitting there doing the same thing. *(Then:)* The story's about a girl who is born blind. Her father's the king and he gets all the kingdom to conspire, so that his daughter will never know that there is such a thing as sight. He does this for the best intentions. She grows up, she's happy, she meets someone; and magically sight is given to her. *(Then:)* In my story, which I keep as a fairy tale, she's now conflicted—thrilled with being able to see; and just as angry that for all this time she'd been told she'd been missing—nothing. *(Then:)* I don't know what it's about. Except—as you say, *that* feeling—that you're missing something. In her case, waking up to the realization that you've missed almost everything. *(Then:)* When I took Benjamin to Lincoln Center to see the tape of his show. His Gaev.

JANE: I'd really like to see that again.

BARBARA: He loved it. Utterly absorbed. Until the end, when the old servant is left behind? And the servant realizes the door is locked from the outside? And he's been forgotten? *(Then:)* Benjamin stopped watching. I asked him why? He said he didn't like that part. What does he know?

(Then:)

JANE: *(Looking* BENJAMIN*)* Will he vote before we take him to Beacon?

BARBARA: I don't know. Is that necessary? Does he have to?

RICHARD: I ask myself the same thing.

MARIAN: Richard…

JANE: We'd have to tell him who to vote for.

MARIAN: He'll vote Democrat.

RICHARD: *(To himself)* Glad that's settled…

MARIAN: That's what he said last night. We watched a little of Obama's last rally—

BARBARA: Until I made her turn it off—

MARIAN: Obama with Bruce Springsteen? And Uncle said he'd vote for him.

JANE: You sure he didn't mean Springsteen? That's what I thought he meant.

(Then:)

JANE: *(To* RICHARD*)* Did you vote absentee, Richard?

(No response)

MARIAN: Did you?

(No response)

MARIAN: *(To* RICHARD*)* Then, Richard, I'll blame you—

JANE: *(Over her)* He's going to win.

MARIAN: Do you really think so?

JANE: He's going to win New York.

RICHARD: I would have voted for Obama. I think I would have. Does that count for something? *(Smiles)*

(Then:)

JANE: I tell myself—and try to convince myself—that voting is like—recycling. I know it doesn't seem to make any difference. What the hell is another coke can more or less? But—for that second, when you're throwing something in the recycling trash—you can feel like you're part of something—greater than yourself. That's what I tell myself. I'm trying to convince myself.

RICHARD: The way I see it now is that most people seem to just want somebody who can articulate their hatreds.

(Then:)

MARIAN: I think we are arguing about important things, Richard. Medicare, Social Security, Ryan—

RICHARD: Shouting. Scaring people. Demonizing.

MARIAN: There are differences, Richard.

(RICHARD shrugs.)

MARIAN: Don't just shrug...

(Pause)

RICHARD: Do we know what *we're* rooting for? I think we know what we're rooting against. And is that enough? Why have we become— "not them"? Oh, but today anyone with doubts must shut up. Save the doubts for tomorrow. I'm sorry. Sorry. I should shut up. "Today" we're interested in—who is going to fucking win. *(Then:)* Because— "today, thank God we're not *them*."

(BENJAMIN makes a noise.)

BARBARA: Just dreaming.

MARIAN: *(To RICHARD)* I want to be more—than just disappointed.

(Then:)

JANE: I want to be useful.

MARIAN: So do something useful, for God's sake.

BARBARA: Marian...

MARIAN: *(To BARBARA)* What a stupid thing to say.

JANE: No one's listening. It's just us. Let me say stupid things, okay? *(Then:)* I voted. Absentee.

MARIAN: Good.

RICHARD: Was that you saying something stupid?

JANE: Something—useful. Something—good. I know how that sounds. I admire Barbara—all she's done—

BARBARA: Don't patronize me.

JANE: I wasn't—

MARIAN: What are you trying to say, Jane? And don't do that to Barbara, you know she hates that.

JANE: I was just reading in a book Tim gave me about a small village in Switzerland. It'd been chosen to be the site of a nuclear waste dump? It does have to go somewhere right? But the villagers have to vote on it first. The government offers them thousands of Swiss francs each. And—they vote "no". Then someone gets what sounds like a crazy idea—to vote again, but this time, offer them nothing. And so they vote, and it passes. I understand that. *(Then:)* When did sacrifice become something foolish? Or have I just woken up to this, and it's always been this way? It's always been— take what you can get. You are an idiot if you don't. God what I must sound like. Glad no one's listening. 'I want to do useful things.' People are starving, Jane. Go feed them.

BARBARA: We understand.

(Then:)

JANE: An important man, who was in the Obama administration. He'd been President of Harvard.

RICHARD: Larry Summers. That's Larry Summers.

JANE: He's quoted in this book, the same book—

MARIAN: As the Swiss village?

JANE: *(Nods)* That Tim wanted me to read. *(Then)* The man says: we have only so much altruism in us. Only so much generosity. So much civic spirit. So we need to think of it as a commodity that gets depleted; and so, he says, you - and I think he means politicians—have to be careful how you ask it to be spent. *(Then:)* I've asked myself this and wanted to ask you. What do you think? Is generosity, is being good, is goodness itself for Christ sake, even love of country—are these all just commodities, goods that can be depleted with use? Or—are they more like muscles that can develop and grow stronger with exercise? And atrophy if not used? *(Then:)* If I could have one minute with our President, I would ask him that. *(Short pause)* Four years ago, I thought he knew the answer. Now?

MARIAN: After four years of being beaten to a pulp by Republicans—

JANE: I hope that's not all he'd say, Marian. I hope to god he wouldn't just say that.

RICHARD: He might.

JANE: I know.

RICHARD: That's what he seems to say—

JANE: I know.

MARIAN: Fox has been on his back, Richard, since the day he was elected. Even before—

RICHARD: And "our" side's better? "We" put Al Sharpton on T V. "Why the fuck not?"

(Short pause)

JANE: I remember being on 86th and Broadway getting on the bus and the black driver putting his hand over where you put your metrocard, and saying—not today, it's free tonight. It was a party.

RICHARD: It won't be like that tonight... No matter
what, it won't be like that tonight. *(Then:)* What would
you ask the President, Marian? If you had a minute
with him?

(Then:)

MARIAN: I'd thank him.

JANE: You would.

RICHARD: For what?

MARIAN: I think he's done his best. I haven't agreed
with everything, sir.

(JANE makes a face.)

MARIAN: I'm not even looking at you. *(Continues to
"the President")* And a lot of things didn't get done that
should have, sir. *(Then:)* And my boyfriend, John--

BARBARA: You're going to tell the President about your
boyfriend?

MARIAN: Why not? It's not a secret anymore.

BARBARA: I don't think he's interested—

MARIAN: *(Continues)* John says that even he has
admired how hard you've worked. But he isn't
voting for you. And we both think you've survived
with integrity in tact, sir. *(To the others)* That's an
accomplishment.

RICHARD: If it's true. *(Then)* Is it true? *(Shrugs)*

MARIAN: When John and I were in Philly visiting *(To
JANE)* your son—by the way did you know he wants to
be called "William" now—

(JANE rolls her eyes.)

MARIAN: John asked if he and his friends felt at all—
disappointed. Some do, he said. One of his friends,
who was staying with him—I asked her—

JANE: "Her"?

MARIAN: A friend. I think. She said, his friend— *(To JANE)* We both liked her. —That it wasn't really a feeling of betrayal. Nothing at all like that. More like the everyday disappointments you have in a long term relationship. *(Smiles)* Of course she wasn't quite old enough to know about long term relationships. But I get it. She said it was part of what she thought growing up meant.

JANE: Being— "sort of" disappointed?

RICHARD: I don't talk enough to young people. I tried during Occupy—that seems like years ago…I remember some kid saying to me, that it was just a natural reaction—anger, angst, scorn at the way things are. The overwhelming sense that things are fucked up—so the only response is to fix it. And so that's what they were trying to do. How? That's what I don't understand. What do they want to do? I couldn't figure that out from being down there then.

BARBARA: My students—. My kids of course are younger, but the older ones also come back. And I see them. They come back and seek me out.

RICHARD: Why am I not surprised.

BARBARA: I asked one of my favorites. She was back from college. Like you, Richard, I was curious. So I asked her: what do young people want now?

RICHARD: And?

BARBARA: Damnit, she said, why separate out the "young people"? She got quite angry with me. Which I liked of course. She said it really pisses her off that people keep emphasizing 'our youthfulness'—that feels to them infantilizing and dismissive. And, she looked right at me—and, she said, it also lets older people off the hook.

(Then:)

JANE: Billy said—

MARIAN: "William."

JANE: *(To* MARIAN*)* I'm his mother. *(Continues)* Billy said something to me. He does talk to me too. Not just to his Aunt and her sexy boyfriend.

MARIAN: *(To* BARBARA*)* I'm glad she thinks he's—

BARBARA: *(Over this, to* MARIAN*)* She hasn't even seen him, Marian. She's making fun of you.

MARIAN: I don't think so.

JANE: *(Continues)* I was going on about the "millennials" or whatever that generation is now called. All this—what looked to me like—just constant self-absorption? Who the hell cares what you ate for lunch? I said it seemed like they were just wasting their lives. To me.

RICHARD: I agree. That's what it looks like.

JANE: Listen to our music, he said. The belief is out there now that anyone can make his own music. Or video. You-tube. And he said isn't that a good thing? Why isn't that a good thing? Isn't it—to use a word you, Mom, always liked to use, he said to me—isn't it—democratic? *(Then:)* Then he said, that in maybe two, three years, or my god maybe ten—he said that like he'd never live to see it… *(Smiles)* In maybe ten years—what now looks to be an inextricable mess, Mom, or what you call "self-absorption" —it's going to be seen as only something we're going through, and after we've gone through it, it will all make sense.

(BENJAMIN *mumbles in his sleep.)*

(BARBARA *leans over and listens.)*

RICHARD: What's he saying?

BARBARA: It sounded like "bullshit".

(They laugh.)

JANE: One night when I was visiting Billy, while I couldn't sleep—Billy was giving me his bed, he slept on the floor. He and I talked. *(Then:)* He said—Mom, let me explain it to you this way. How I see the country. *(Then:)* It's like two divorcing parents, Mom. Like you and Dad. And they hate each other. They're screaming at each other. They're certainly not talking and listening to each other. And they both turn to their son and they say to him—who's right, son? They shout at him: Damnit, son, you need to take a side! They scream at him: Take a goddamn side! *(Then:)* But the son says, I can't. I won't take a fucking side. Can't you and Dad understand what I'm trying to tell you? I don't want to be like either of you...

(Then:)

RICHARD: How did we get talking about our children? It's election day. *(Then, the answer)* Because it's election day.

MARIAN: On Evan's i-Pod...it took me about six months after Evan died... After she killed herself... That's the first time I think I've been able to say those words.

(MARIAN looks to BARBARA.)

BARBARA: I never heard you say it.

(Then:)

MARIAN: Six months after—for me to really listen to—the songs on her i-Pod. To really hear them.

BARBARA: *(Smiles, teasing)* Now it's all she listens to.

MARIAN: That's not true. *(Then)* Really listen. And hear them. She had good taste. I'm learning her taste. It's so strange to hear some of these young women singers...

They sound like kids. Little girl voices. They are kids.
There's one I keep listening to. I'm sure you don't
know her. *(Then:)* I've played it for Barbara. It starts:
"They made a statue of us." And this young female
child-like and so innocent voice, she sounds so proud.
"And put it on a mountaintop." "Where tourists come
and stare at us." "Blow bubbles with their gum, take
photographs for fun." Then a swell of strings: "They'll
name a city after us!" *(Then)* "And later say it's all our
fault." "Then they'll give us a talking to. They'll give
us a talking to, because they have years of experience."
The latter is sung with just dripping distain. "Years of
experience". Then, "we're living in a den of thieves".
Which she repeats over and over. Until, she just sings:
"it's contagious." "It's contagious."

(Then:)

JANE: If *I* could have another minute with the
President.

(All interested in this)

JANE: I'd tell him what Billy said recently to me. Mom,
I think mine is a lost generation. We're doing shit
jobs, and not being trained for anything. And when
the economy gets better, it's the younger ones they're
going to want to train then. He's twenty-two years old.
And he and his friends think they've been forgotten.

(Then:)

MARIAN: What about you, Richard? If you had one
minute with the President. What would you say to
him?

(RICHARD thinks. Then:)

RICHARD: President Obama or President Romney?

MARIAN: Jesus—

RICHARD: Which one?

MARIAN: *(Over this)* That can't happen. I'd move to Canada.

JANE: No you won't.

RICHARD: Dear President Obama,

(They all listen.)

RICHARD: How did you, the voice of our better selves, begin appealing to our hates? How did that happen? How? *(Then:)* Do you accept any responsibility for that? *(Then:)* And are you sorry?

MARIAN: That's not fair, Richard.

JANE: If it's what he feels… Anyway who's listening? And I doubt if he's the only one who feels like that today.

BARBARA: Romney—Richard. Just in case he wins. Say a fluke.

JANE: I'm not sure he needs a fluke—

(They all wait, then:)

RICHARD: Dear President Romney: *(Then:)* Well, Nixon went to China. So there's that sort of hope. But if this really is all about helping your rich friends; if you are scamming us. If you really see us just as the heavy baggage to be tossed overboard to keep the ship sailing smooth and fast. If those who are saying this now, warning us—turn out to be correct, sir. Then—God have mercy on your soul…

JANE: And Barbara? What would you like to say, to either one?

(Then:)

BARBARA: I suppose I'd tell them both that I sort of stopped paying attention a while back. Sorry. *(Then:)* And then I think I'd ask them—you both spent how much on this election? I think I read—two billion dollars. Maybe I'm wrong but it seems to me, it was mostly spent—scaring people about the other guy. And so now—look what you've got—a whole lot of people who are very scared...

(Then:)

(Lights fade.)

Sorrow and its Beauty

(A short time later. MARIAN holds some pieces of paper.)

(BENJAMIN is still asleep at the card table.)

JANE: I should get dressed...

MARIAN: I need to vote. *(She starts to pick up plates, etc.)*

BARBARA: Leave it. Leave it. We'll do all that later.

MARIAN: Has some alien taken over our sister's body?

BARBARA: Shut up.

JANE: *(Getting up)* What time are we expected in Beacon?

MARIAN: Anytime after ten.

RICHARD: *(To Jane as she starts to go)* Where have you been sleeping?

JANE: With Marian. *(She makes a face.)*

MARIAN: Why do you make a face? What are you saying?

(JANE goes.)

Barbara, what is she talking about? *(To RICHARD)* She's the one thrashing around...

RICHARD: *(To BARBARA)* It's all going to be for the best.

MARIAN: *(To BARBARA)* Listen to Richard. *(She kisses RICHARD on the cheek. Quietly)* I'm going to go and vote.

BARBARA: Do that, Marian. Do that.

MARIAN: I'm so glad you're here, Richard. *(Then: To* BARBARA*)* Are you going to vote? *(Then about* RICHARD*)* Don't listen to him. *(She goes.)*

BARBARA: "John" is poll watching.

RICHARD: You said.

BARBARA: That's why she wants to—

RICHARD: I figured.

BARBARA: Marian's put her contacts in. *(She stands and heads to the table to pick up.)*

RICHARD: Hey, I thought you said to leave it.

*(*BARBARA *sits at the table.)*

RICHARD: I realized recently—. Something I used to do as a kid. I remembered when I was in England.

BARBARA: What's that?

RICHARD: I don't think I ever told anybody this. I used to—draw lines between things.

BARBARA: What??

RICHARD: In my head, my mind. Between say the edge of the table here to that chair. And then—I'd cross the line. And then draw another. And I'd cross that. And another. I'd forgotten about doing that. Then I found myself doing it again. In London. I suppose, it gives you the illusion that you're moving forward. *(Then:)* It's the right thing to do.

BARBARA: For him or for us, Richard? *(Then:)* I could— can—still take care of him. I'm not scared of what he might do.

RICHARD: I think you are. And I think that's fine. I'm going to stay the night. Is that okay?

BARBARA: Of course. They're saying another storm's coming tomorrow.

RICHARD: I'll risk it. Can I have Benjamin's bed? Think about it. *(Then:)* I'm going to follow Marian to the polls.

BARBARA: You can't vote here.

RICHARD: I want to see what "John" looks like. *(Smiles)*

BARBARA: He's not very handsome. That's not a nice thing to say. Sorry. He's okay.

RICHARD: Marian really needs someone, don't you think? I'm glad she's found someone. You should find someone too.

(BARBARA stares at RICHARD.)

RICHARD: Now you won't have any excuse... *(Then:)* That came out harsher than I meant. I'm sorry, Barbara. *(He quickly goes.)*

(Pause)

(BARBARA looks at BENJAMIN. He wakes up.)

BENJAMIN: What time is it?

BARBARA: Seven in the morning. Richard and Marian are coming back. Jane's getting dressed. *(She picks up.)* Earlier Benjamin, you were dreaming. I wonder what you were dreaming about.

BENJAMIN: I don't know.

BARBARA: We often forget our dreams. I know I always do. *(She has picked up some folded pages off the table.)*

BENJAMIN: What's that, Barbara?

BARBARA: For your talent show. You read it to us last night.

BENJAMIN: What talent show?

(As BARBARA hands BENJAMIN the pages; and continues to straighten up:)

BARBARA: I've told you about it. You were excited about it. Jane said how much she loved hearing you read that tonight...

BENJAMIN: *(As he looks at the papers)* I don't remember this.

BARBARA: *(Explaining)* He's in prison. He's writing his lover. It's just the end of the letter... They told me it couldn't be more than a few minutes long. *(Smiles)*

(BENJAMIN is reading it to himself.)

(BARBARA picks up.)

BARBARA: *(Noticing this)* Out loud, Uncle. Read it out loud. It's good practice. It's always good to practice. *(As she straightens up:)*

BENJAMIN: *(Reads)* "I am to be released toward the end of May. I tremble with pleasure when I think both laburnum and the lilac will be blooming in the gardens—." *(He looks up.)*

BARBARA: Yes. We have lilacs in our garden, Benjamin. *(She sits and listens.)*

BENJAMIN: *(Continues)* "—and that I shall see the wind stir into restless beauty the swaying gold of the one, and make the other toss the pale purple of its plumes so that all the air shall be Arabia for me."

(JANE enters, and sits down to listen.)

BENJAMIN: "It is always twilight in one's cell, where it is always midnight in one's heart.

"I have lain in prison for nearly two years. Out of my nature has come wild despair: an abandonment to grief; terrible and impotent rage; anguish that wept aloud: misery that could find no voice: sorrow that was dumb. I have passed through every possible mood of suffering. But something tells me that nothing in the whole world is meaningless, and suffering least of all. *That* something hidden away in my nature, like a treasure in a field, is Humility. It is the last thing left in me, and the best. And of all things it is the strangest.

"The gods had given me almost everything. I had genius. I made art a philosophy, and philosophy an art. I summed up all systems in a phrase, and all existence in an epigram.

"And as such—you came to me. I think to learn the Pleasure of Life and the Pleasure of Art. Perhaps now—I am chosen to teach you something much more wonderful: the meaning of Sorrow, and its beauty.

"Your affectionate friend,

Oscar Wilde."

(Then:)

BARBARA: *(To say something, to* JANE*)* That sweater looks nice. I'll wear my scarf later. That'll make Richard happy...

JANE: Where is Richard?

BARBARA: He went to see what "John" looked like. *(She goes to* BENJAMIN*.)* That was very good, Uncle. *(Kisses him on the cheek.)*

*(*JANE *watches this, then:)*

JANE: Maybe I'll go see what "John" looks like too. She said he's not very handsome.

BARBARA: *(Smiles to herself)* Did she?

JANE: *(Starting to go)* Are we taking two cars?

BENJAMIN: Are we going somewhere?

*(*BARBARA *looks to* JANE *to explain.)*

JANE: For a drive, Uncle. *(She hesitates going.)*

BARBARA: *(Suddenly)* Jane, stay with Benjamin for a moment.

(BARBARA *hurries off into the living room.*)

(*Short pause*)

JANE: I remember you reading that at the Y, Uncle. The first thing you did in public, after your—heart attack. We were all there. I remember Richard saying it was like you'd never been ill. (*Then:*) I'll bet you win that talent show.

(BARBARA *hurries back out of breath with a small framed photo and a dog collar.*)

JANE: I won't be long... (*She goes.*)

(BARBARA *and* BENJAMIN *look at each other, she shows him what she's brought.*)

BARBARA: I wanted to make sure you had these with you. Okay?

BENJAMIN: What??

BARBARA: (*Handing it to him*) It's a dog collar. I want to make sure you put this on your nightstand. It was your dog's. His name was Oliver.

BENJAMIN: (*Takes the collar, examines it*) Oliver. I don't remember Oliver.

BARBARA: I know. (*Then she tries to hand him the photo.*) And this is a photo of me. You keep it on your bureau. Will you do that? Please. It'll make me happy.

BENJAMIN: I don't understand—

BARBARA: You will. Please. Keep it.

(BENJAMIN *takes it. Looks at the photo, then looks at* BARBARA.)

(*He takes her hand; he kisses it. She moves away from him.*)

BENJAMIN: What's wrong? Barbara, have I done something wrong?

(BARBARA *looks at* BENJAMIN, *then goes to the puzzle.*)

BARBARA: *(About the puzzle)* Are we really going to do this puzzle? Let's put it away. I'd rather it wasn't out when we came back… *(She starts to put the pieces of the puzzle back in the puzzle box.)*

BENJAMIN: Why? I like it.

(BENJAMIN goes to BARBARA. She stops picking up the puzzle.)

BARBARA: *(About the picture on the box)* Look at this girl, Uncle. What is *she* thinking?

BENJAMIN: Barbara?

(BARBARA moves away from BENJAMIN and goes to the table "to clean up", but sits. He sits at the puzzle.)

BARBARA: Jane and Tim are going to move to Rhinebeck, Benjamin.

BENJAMIN: *(Beginning to do the puzzle)* That'll be nice for us. *(Smiles. Then:)* Who's Tim?

BARBARA: *(Picking up)* You've met Tim, many times… He's Jane's boyfriend. He's an actor. Like you. You like him.

BENJAMIN: *(Doing the puzzle)* An actor…

(Then:)

BARBARA: Marian has a boyfriend. That's very good. I'm so happy for her.

(BENJAMIN nods.)

BARBARA: So Richard's back from England. That's nice. I'm sure Pamela—that's his wife—is happy about that. And their kids. He was gone for a long time. He seems—at loose ends, didn't you think? We all saw that. But didn't say anything about it. *(Smiles at BENJAMIN)* I've been worried about him. We all were. We know how he can just shut himself away. Without his family around…

(Church bells toll seven in the distance. BARBARA *looks at her watch, then:)*

BARBARA: *(To* BENJAMIN*)* I'll vote later...

*(*BARBARA *and* BENJAMIN *sit.)*

END OF PLAY

NOTE

SORRY is the third play in a four-play series about the Apple Family, set in Rhinebeck, New York, my home. Like each of the first two plays, SORRY was written to open on the day it is set, Tuesday, November 6, 2012 or election day.

In notes to each of the first two plays, I have raised the issue of these being "disposable" plays; that is, plays so anchored in their specific time as to be soon out of date. That may indeed be the case, though I have begun to hope it isn't so. In fact, it is now my ambition to put the four plays together once they have all been written and performed, to make, what I hope will be, a very long, but also coherent play—one which, though set on four very specific days, also charts this family over four difficult years. Difficult for the family, as well as, I believe, for our country. We'll see if this happens, and if the sum can be greater than the parts. I really don't know.

This is now the third play with the same characters on the same set (only Tim is absent here). But what is not immediately apparent reading the play is that this is the third play with the *same* actors playing the same characters on the same set. As I have also directed these plays, I have to say what a unique experience this has been; often on the first day of rehearsal, actors are just getting to know each other, and the long journey of making an ensemble begins. Here, on the first day, they are not just an ensemble, but like a real family. And, this writer has begun to cross a line between writing characters and uncovering people whom he sees before him. In other words, I have now begun to use the personalities, the complexities, the confusions of the people who are acting in these plays to help me probe the depth of the characters themselves.

Earlier this year I opened a play called FAREWELL TO THE THEATRE in London; its central character is the playwright, director, actor, theater visionary Harley Granville Barker. In that play I have Barker speak words he wrote in his essay, 'The Heritage of the Actor':

"One is tempted to imagine a play—to be written in desperate defiance of Aristotle—from which *doing* would be eliminated altogether, in which nothing but *being* would be left. The task set the actors would be to interest their audience in what the characters *were*, quite apart from anything they might *do*; to set up, that is to say, the relation by which all important human intimacies exist."

I'm learning more and more that this is an ambition of these Apple Family plays; to put characters in a room with an audience, who then can watch them *be*. To where the private thoughts of the characters, derived often from the very actors playing them, work to make the relation between actor and audience as intimate as relations in real life. To let the audience not only share the same space, but find themselves inside the characters' minds. In other words, to create 'the relation by which all important human intimacies exist."

And so as I wrote in the note to SWEET AND SAD, it is my hope that these plays are about the need to talk, the

need to listen, the need for theatre, *and,* I now add, the
need to be in the same room together.

Numerous books and articles influenced the writing
of SORRY: Oliver Sack's *The Mind's Eye, A History
of Private Life,* General Editors: Philippe Aries and
Georges Duby *(volumes II, III & IV);* Roy Franklin
Nichols' *Franklin Pierce: Young Hickory of the Granite
Hills;* Nathaniel Hawthorne's *Life of Franklin Pierce;
Occupy! Scenes from Occupied America,* edited by
Astra Taylor, Keith Cassen and the editors from *n+1;*
essays by David Brooks, Charles M Blow and Michael
Winerip *('On Education')* in *The New York Times.* My
daughter, Jocelyn, and her friends, Evan, Mat, Holly,
Margaret, Sarah, Adrienne and Hilary, supplied me
with invaluable insight into a younger generation's
take on Occupy Wall Street, President Obama, and so
much more; my friend Oliver Cotton (unwittingly)
supplied the anecdote about making the film about
Columbus; the book Richard was reading on the plane
home is Julian Barnes' *The Sense of an Ending;* and the
edit and re-ordering of Oscar Wilde's *De Profundis* was
adapted from a version originally edited by Merlin
Holland. The book Barbara has been reading and from
which she quotes is: Michael J Sandel's brilliant *What
Money Can't Buy.* The song Evan had on her i-pod is
Regina Spektor's *Us.* The story about the urinals and
the fish comes from *Tynan,* a play adapted by me with
Colin Chambers from *The Diaries of Kenneth Tynan.*

And as with THAT HOPEY CHANGEY THING and
SWEET AND SAD, SORRY is a work of fiction, and not
based upon any living person or persons.

R N/Rhinebeck